SLAY
YOUR
OWN
DRAGONS

SLAY YOUR OWN DRAGONS

*How Women Can Overcome
Self-Sabotage in Love and Work*

NANCY GOOD

ST. MARTIN'S PRESS
NEW YORK

Design by Fearn Cutler

Library of Congress Cataloging-in-Publication Data

Good, Nancy.
    Slay your own dragons : how women can overcome self-sabotage in love and work / Nancy Good.
        p.   cm.
    ISBN 0-312-03935-2
    1. Women—Psychology.   2. Self-destructive behavior.   I. Title.
HQ1206.G68   1990
155.6'33—dc20   89-24341

First Edition
10 9 8 7 6 5 4 3 2 1

CONTENTS

▲▲▲▲▲▲▲▲▲▲▲▲▲▲▲▲▲▲▲▲▲▲▲▲

ACKNOWLEDGMENTS

JUST a few brief words of thanks to those who helped with their support, encouragement, and advice throughout the long process of writing this book. Thanks to Mildred Moskowitz, Lena Furgeri, Lou Levy, Ursula Brown, Louis Ormont, Aimee Levy, Ceil Berlin, Bruce Hertz, Debra Hertz, and my parents. Most important, thanks to my husband, Wendell Craig, whose love and caring remain unflinching through life's (and this book's) trials and tribulations.

A special thank you goes to my editor, Toni Lopopolo, for her guidance and persistence; her ideas about structure helped the book to attain its final form. Thanks also to my agent, Agnes Birnbaum, to Aileen Spinner for her help on the addictions segment, and to Eva Chertov, who shared with me her ideas about dragons.

My appreciation to all.

FOREWORD

Dragons and Self-Sabotage
▼▼▼▼▼▼▼▼▼▼▼▼▼▼▼▼▼▼▼▼▼▼▼▼▼▼▼▼▼▼▼▼▼▼▼▼▼▼

A woman who came to see me a few years ago told me about her "dragons." No, they weren't some exotic new pets; this was the name she gave the thoughts she had about herself that made her miserable. Her dragons were negative tapes that played in her head, preventing her from being everything she wanted to be and having everything she wanted to have. I thought "dragons" was the perfect name to give these self-sabotaging thoughts we all carry around with us.

Dragons traditionally destroyed beauty. They demanded and devoured virgins, burned the countryside with their fiery breath, killed handsome young men, and were repulsively ugly. Similarly, women destroy their tremendous potential and inner beauty because their dragons—their destructive emotional voices—get loose in their heads.

I realized quite some time ago that no knight in shining armor can slay these dragons for you. But you can learn to slay your own dragons. This book will give you the skills you'll need to end self-sabotage forever.

SLAY
YOUR
OWN
DRAGONS

CHAPTER 1

▼▼▼▼▼▼▼▼▼▼▼▼▼▼▼▼▼▼▼

OVERVIEW

▲▲▲▲▲▲▲▲▲▲▲▲▲▲▲▲▲▲▲▲▲▲▲

*Women and Self-Sabotage on
the Brink of Love and Success*

▼▼▼

SUE is a graduate of a prestigious medical school and heads her own family clinic. Even though she desperately wants to get married, she enters into affairs with already-married or otherwise unavailable men.

Laura is an award-winning violinist, recently married. Since the wedding she has become so chronically tired and ill that she has had to put her career on hold.

June received a scholarship for her artistic ability in college. Four years later she is in a dead-end job, underpaid and unappreciated. She makes no move to change jobs. Her boyfriend mistreats her, but she does nothing about that either.

What do these three women have in common? Each is the unknowing victim of a syndrome that has ruined the lives of too many terrific women. I call this syndrome "unconscious self-sabotage on the brink of love or success." It has halted all of us at some time or another in work or love, though fortunately most of are affected only temporarily. But for some of us the effects have been far more drastic. Sue, Laura, and June are all intelligent enough to overcome their problems, but unconscious inner conflicts about love and work are holding them back, ultimately causing them to commit self-sabotage.

If you find that small problems endlessly trouble you or that large ones rob you of happiness, unconscious self-sabotage may be at work. There may be a pattern to the problems that have been keeping you from reaching the goals you've struggled to reach, goals involving love or success and the emotional and physical health you must have to enjoy both. The problems that deprive you of what you want can be minor, like twisting an ankle before a hiking vacation you've planned, or major, as in the case of the woman who says she wants to marry but gets involved only with married lovers. The ways in which you sabotage yourself can be obvious, such as "forgetting" to send your résumé to a company with an exciting new job possibility, or buying a beautiful new wardrobe and then gaining weight because of a food addiction, or constantly putting yourself in debt because of compulsive overspending. Or they can be hidden, as with a woman who is constantly depressed and anxious all the time so that she cannot enjoy the good things in her life.

All of the many women I've known as a psychotherapist, including myself, have experienced misfortunes of some sort just as we were on the brink of "having it all." None of us deliberately tried to be self-destructive or planned job. For example, you take a lower-paying boring job instead of trying for the higher-paying more challenging one. And fear of failure stops many women in their tracks. If you never get the right man or the right job, you don't have to fear being rejected or fired, but you keep busy by failing over and over.

Whatever your particular reasons may be for preventing yourself from having a satisfying romantic relationship or a fulfilling career or both, self-sabotage is painful and frustrating. You don't *feel* that you brought any of this on yourself, and blaming yourself is the last thing you want or need to do. Yet when we think *self-sabotage*, we also think "I'm at fault," "I'm bad," "I've done the wrong thing again." Fortunately, you can change this negative way of thinking.

HOW TO CLOSE THE DOOR ON SELF-BLAME

Children learn early on that if, say, chocolate milk is spilled on the floor, this is "bad," and if they caused it, they are also bad and at fault. If you were treated this way by parents or others, then it is only a quick moment to an adulthood in which you continue to blame yourself because you hate your job but can't find the energy to change careers, or because you haven't found a man, or because you're with a man but you're unhappy. You even hate yourself when you complain about your predicament.

Understanding yourself and being sympathetic to yourself, while at the same time watching for the causes of your problems, is not a skill most people are ever taught. But it can be learned. In order to understand why you sabotage yourself, you must eliminate self-blame from your thoughts. Why? Because self-blame stifles self-understanding. As we proceed through these chapters, you will have a greater chance to avoid self-blame and overcome self-sabotage if you tell yourself:

▶ Your self-sabotage is due to unconscious causes. You are not aware in those moments that you are sabotaging yourself, so therefore blame is pointless.

▶ Your personal forms of self-sabotage were originally caused by sources other than yourself—family, teachers, and all kinds of social and cultural pressures. There are definite causes behind your actions that you are not responsible for.

▶ You must not blame yourself when you see that you are being self-destructive. It will not help. Only self-awareness and understanding will help.

▶ We all sabotage ourselves to some degree; it takes courage to be willing to face this. Give yourself credit for facing your "dragons" and "slaying" them.

Now I hope you can proceed to learn about self-sabotage without thinking you're "bad." One way that you can assess whether you have begun to blame yourself is to monitor your anxiety level. If you feel an increase in anxiety—you feel a headache coming on, you want to stop reading, your palms are sweaty—you are beginning to think your self-sabotage is your fault. If you feel excessively anxious as you read, return to the four points listed above to avoid self-blame before proceeding.

Mary, the first of the talented women we will look at in these chapters, had an experience with a client that provides a good example of how to see your problems realistically without blaming yourself, and how to find solutions.

Mary is an artist who has her own business designing advertisements. Her problem is that she never seems to make enough money, although she works all the time. Recently, however, instead of just complaining, she decided to look at what she might be doing to cause her financial problem. During a phone conversation, Mary realized that she once again had negotiated a price too low for the wonderful work she'd done. She did not blame herself and get depressed, as she might have. Instead she thought clearly about the conversation and remembered that actually she had told the client that she could reduce her price before he had asked about it.

Mary saw that she was causing her own financial problems, but she was also aware of her reasons. She was nervous because she didn't have many clients. She also realized that her parents had never encouraged her to make money. If anything, her father always seemed to enjoy it when she called home to ask for money. Although she was upset that she had sabotaged herself by volunteering to lower her price, she was determined to learn to state her fee without acting on her anxiety.

She decided that night to role-play negotiating fees, with the help of a friend who was willing to play a tough client. Mary was able to stick to her guns each time by remembering how a former boss had handled this. She asked for more than she expected to get and bargained down. She used her new skill on her next client—and it worked! She also used this technique with her boyfriend, who always wanted his way, and she got her way for a change.

When she recognized how she sabotaged herself, and why, Mary saw that she could eventually have control over how much money she made, and maybe even over how men treated her, as well. When you stop finding fault with yourself, you can guard against self-sabotage, just as Mary did. It's a skill you too can master.

SELF-SABOTAGE "ON THE BRINK"

Before any battle, a general makes sure he knows the enemy well: his habits, strategies, and weaknesses. Similarly, you must know your own internal "enemies"—the forces of self-sabotage—as well as you know the other, more accessible aspects of yourself. The definition of *sabotage* clarifies this: "to destroy or render useless; the . . . damaging of machinery or materials or disruption of work by dissatisfied workmen or hostile agents." Thus, when you sabotage yourself, you render a part of yourself useless, a part of yourself that might give and receive love, achieve financial success and creative fulfillment. In fact, your "machinery" is being damaged by hostile agents—those voices inside you from the past that convince the otherwise healthy you to be self-destructive.

Therapists call these voices *introjects*. They are unconsciously recorded recollections of past criticisms, which have become stuck in your memory and affect your actions today. During those situations when you might sabotage yourself, your positive voices battle your negative voices, your introjects, for control. Yet most of the decisions we make in life, the things we say, the actions we take—we do most of this by rote, out of habit.

You are probably not aware of negative or positive "tapes" playing in your head as you live day to day, but they are there all the same. That is why the very first step in overcoming self-sabotage is self-observation. Like any scientist, you must first observe the subject—you—objectively. Then look at the situation and the thoughts that caused you to "damage your machinery." (And keep in mind that the damage we cause ourselves through self-sabotage *is* almost always reversible.) Don't be afraid to acknowledge that you have set yourself back; it's all part of the learning process.

To be on the brink of any kind of event creates excitement that is laced with anxiety, tension, and stress. For many reasons, which we will explore in later chapters, the time when you are on the "brink" of love or of success in your work is a dangerous period, a time when self-sabotage is most likely to occur. Recognizing when you are on the brink takes effort and practice. It is not always obvious. You may be on the brink of love, although you have not even met *the* man, because emotionally you are different, truly ready to make a commitment with the right person this time. When you are offered a better-paying, more rewarding job, you are on the brink as well. Being on the brink can also include that period just after love or success has come your way when the feelings that rise up can trigger self-sabotage if you are unaware.

Most important, however, as a terrific woman you are *always* on the brink of love or success because you are capable of having so much at any time—once you *overcome self-sabotage*. In the following chapters we will look at women who have gone through a lifetime of self-sabotage and were still able to overcome their self-destructive habits. Josie and Susan are two women who were on the brink of love and success. They came close to self-sabotage but stopped themselves because they were willing to observe closely how they behaved.

Josie was a sweet-looking woman with an outstanding level of energy. You felt this when you met her. She was never tired after working at her job as a buyer for a chain of gift stores and also running her own company. She bought and made handcrafted items and sold her own sweaters, rugs, and other items at weekend fairs. She had many women friends and occasionally dated, but at the age of thirty-one she had never been in a long-term romantic relationship. This had only begun to bother her in the past year. It had been bothering her mother for much longer than that.

Josie decided to turn some of her energy toward examining herself in hopes of figuring out why a relationship

eluded her. She had never felt especially excited about the
men she met; they must have felt the same way about her.
Before her thirtieth birthday she'd told herself that it was
bad luck or that her time had not yet come, but now she
began to think about why and how she might be sabotaging
herself. Although her mother said how much she wanted
Josie to get married, Josie began to think that that could
not be the whole truth. Her mother had been alone since
Josie's father died a few years before, and she relied heavily
on Josie for companionship and chores. Josie would not be
right there all the time if a man came into her life, and this
would definitely upset her mother. Josie also saw that her
parents' relationship—her father was "king" and Mom lived
to serve him—was one that Josie was afraid she would
duplicate. Once Josie was willing to consider that she was
sabotaging herself, many other reasons for the sabotage
became apparent. She began to observe how she avoided
a relationship and began to monitor her feelings. She noticed that when she was with a man on a date, she was
actually brimming with feelings: she felt scared, anxious,
angry, and impatient to get home. The way she acted,
however, was quite different. She got quiet and cold in her
responses.

The next few times she met a man, she continued to
observe this in herself. One evening at a party she made
a special effort to act more warmly and enjoyed herself more
than she usually did. She was at first pleased when one of
the men she had met called her. Then she noticed that for
no reason, she could feel herself thinking that he was a
jerk. She recognized that this was the same negative tape
that always played in her head. Since Josie had taken a
major step, she decided not to listen to these negative
"voices" and instead accepted the date. She would give this
man a chance. She knew that this self-monitoring and self-
understanding would be a constant struggle for her. How-

ever, she felt now that finding a good relationship was a far more real possibility than it had been before, whether with this new man or someone else.

Susan was not an assertive woman. She kept quiet at work because she felt so unsure of herself. Even so, because she was extremely bright, it was not long before she was asked if she wanted to learn to handle some accounts at the stockbroker's office where she was a clerk. This was in fact why she had taken the job there. She said yes.

Right away, however, Susan felt that she was in over her head. There was constant pressure to make decisions, and everything happened in a rush all the time. She cried at home, where her fiancé patiently listened and told her she could do it. She didn't believe him. He became angry with her and told her that either she should quit—as she had her previous job, for the same reason—or she should figure out why she was so insecure about herself. She decided to do the latter. Susan had to struggle to look at herself without blaming herself, because she put herself down every chance she got. But she wanted so much to succeed this time that she was able to be objective. Susan understood that the other people at the stockbroker's office weren't really better than she was. Susan thought however that she was "slow" and unsophisticated. This kind of thinking made her workday unbearable, although in reality she did quite well.

The next step was for Susan to understand where these destructive thoughts came from. She decided to try therapy. During a session she remembered that the nuns who had taught her in elementary school had said that she was slow. But Susan also realized that the chaos at home during those years had made it impossible for her to concentrate on her homework. With her parents' arguments, their separations, and her father's criticisms of her, she was lucky to get through those years at all. The most attention she got from them was when she came home with another bad report card. Susan became aware that when she doubted her own abilities, she was "back home" with her father and hoping deep down to get some of that parental attention —not a good kind, but better than nothing. With this awareness of her self-sabotage and its causes, she kept at the job and soon became a full stockbroker, doing well despite her negative "tapes."

You can see how close Josie and Susan came to falling into the pattern of sabotaging themselves in love and work yet again. But their desire for change forced them to think about self-sabotage without self-blame, thus saving them from being self-destructive. Both women had to struggle with recurring bouts of all their destructive feelings and thoughts, as with a flu that keeps returning. Josie did of course at times become cold with men and push them away. Susan did continue to have bouts of self-doubt. But despite occasional steps backward, they eventually got what they wanted.

You have probably heard that you have to take one step back before going forward, but you may be perplexed to hear that this is good for you. Sigmund Freud called this "regression in the service of the ego." Your ego is the part of you that deals with the environment every day. It cannot adapt to totally new ways all at once. It must rest, go back for a time to old habits, which are easier because they're more familiar. This is regression that is helpful for you. For instance, when you sleep all weekend after working hard for weeks, this is a form of regression. Although you may wonder if you are sick, far from being ill, you are recovering from the exhaustion you've brought on yourself; you are resting emotionally and physically by regressing to a sleep pattern that babies usually follow. So this kind of regression is an emotional rest. When you follow old self-destructive habits after a successful "up" period, it means that your old self needed a rest from the strain of new ways of behaving.

But how can you tell if you are just resting or in a bad slump? You can tell the difference if you imagine the last year of your life as a graph. If despite ups and downs, overall the graph of your life is moving upward, then the down points are just resting spots or regression periods. If your imaginary graph is downhill overall, it's an indication of self-sabotage.

LOCATING YOUR ITP—YOUR INDIVIDUAL TURNOFF POINT

You have probably heard these words said about a friend or an acquaintance or even about yourself: "And everything was just going so well when . . ."; "She was just about to [get married, have a family, be promoted, open a business] and then . . ." What follows is usually a description of some type of problem or stumbling block—an illness, an explosive argument, a complication that totally disrupts the upward movement of that person's life. Although the events seem random, the result of "bad luck," there is nothing accidental about them. The woman has, without knowing it, reached her individual turnoff point, or ITP. Your individual turnoff point can be defined as the level of fulfillment in love or the amount of money or fame more than which, deep down, you feel you don't deserve. Each woman's ITP is, as it sounds, unique to her.

Sally, for example, reached her ITP the evening she was supposed to read aloud a short story she had written, to a group of writers in the course she was taking. Her anxiety was so great that she couldn't speak. She stopped

writing after this incident. And that, unfortunately and unnecessarily, is often the case. A talented and deserving
woman arrives at what ought to be an exciting landmark
and jumping-off place, which instead turns into a stopping
point. Up until the incident at the writing course, Sally had
been writing regularly, hoping to get published. She did
well at her job in public relations and had never before
experienced an anxiety attack. When this happened, she
was so shocked at herself and unprepared to deal with her
feelings that she felt she had no alternative but to steer
clear of her dream to be a published writer, so she might
also steer clear of that awful anxiety.

Sally did not feel deep down that she deserved to have
more success and fulfillment in life than she already had.
Each woman has an individual turnoff point determined by
many forces, external and internal. Perhaps you have met
a man but somehow, for some combination of reasons, marriage never occurs. Or you may date many men, but a long-
term relationship doesn't happen. In the first case, your
turnoff point is evidently reached when marriage becomes
a possibility; in the other, your ITP concerns long-term
relationships. But arrival at your ITP does not have to sig-
nal the end of growth for you. Although you may slow
yourself down in some form when you reach your individual
turnoff point, you can overcome this backward pull or emotional paralysis if you are willing to admit that you have a
psychological turnoff point and know where it is.

For instance, Sally does not know how scared she is of
having her stories published. She also does not know how
angry she is that someone has not already seen their merit.
She has fantasies about being discovered. And she has no
idea that her mother's lack of success is one of the reasons
she had an anxiety attack and arrived at her ITP the night
she was to read her story. Forewarned is of course forearmed; once you are willing to be aware that you have a

turnoff point and that you are approaching it, you need not be caught in a state of psychological paralysis.

Thus far we have only seen how an individual turnoff point can be reached *before* you get what you want. However, you may discover that your ITP is reached *after* you get what you want. Success or love comes into your life, and suddenly everything goes wrong. Another way in which you can use the concept of an individual turnoff point, then, is to be aware that any time you finally get what has been frustratingly out of reach for a very long time, this achievement is at the boundary of your ITP, and you have crossed over into wonderful but potentially dangerous territory. With the suggestions given in these pages, however, you can surely battle these destructive forces and keep what is yours.

RATING YOUR SELF-SABOTAGE POTENTIAL

The following questions are designed to help you assess whether or not you are in danger of sabotaging yourself, and where exactly are your emotional weak links that could give way under pressure. (A yes answer indicates a danger zone.) For instance, you may not have realized, as suggested in question one, that worrying more about other people than about yourself can lead to a life of losing out. Women especially have been taught that this is the nice way to be, but it can become an avenue for self-sabotage. As you answer the questions, be careful not to blame yourself for your yes answers. And answer yes only if the situation has occurred repeatedly, not just once.

1. Do you worry more about other people's well-being than about your own?
2. Do you say yes to requests from friends, colleagues, men, children, family, more than you really want to?

3. Are you ready to give others help with their romantic or work problems but are rarely or never able to admit that you need help?

4. Do you usually blame yourself when a problem occurs, whether it is in your romantic life or at work?

5. Do your devalue the things that you have or the good things that happen to you when other people praise you? Do you feel embarrassed or humiliated by praise?

6. Do you seem to get sick just when things are going well or when something good is about to happen?

7. When you are ill, are you secretly relieved to be away from demands and pressures?

8. Do recurring physical ailments interfere with your sex life? Are you secretly relieved?

9. Has an eruption of your anger caused the loss of employment for you more than once?

10. Have you ended work, romantic, or social relationships in a huff more than once? Would your pride be offended if you went back to talk things over quietly?

11. Do you usually think that you're right if there's a problem, and that the other person must be wrong?

12. Have you lost out in love or work because of the suppression of your anger and/or needs?

13. Do you feel deep down that you're not that smart or talented and will never make it? That everyone else is better?

14. Do you feel that you're not with a man, or with the right man, because you're not attractive enough, slim enough, smart enough, clever enough?

If some of these questions apply to you, then you are sabotaging yourself to a greater or lesser degree. Your destructive attitudes have developed unconsciously due to a variety of pressures, some of them felt over the years by all women, some special to your life. Like any pioneer, your willingness to venture into the unexplored territory of your self-sabotage, to understand what has happened and why, takes courage and strength. Once you do understand, however, you will be many steps ahead in claiming the territory that is rightfully yours.

BUT WHY TALK ABOUT WOMEN?
AREN'T MEN WORSE?
AND DON'T THEY SABOTAGE US ALL THE TIME?

Looking at today's society, men seem far more self-destructive than women. But that is not the reality. Although men commit more crimes, make wars, go bankrupt, and have extramarital affairs more than women do—to name just a few of the forms of self-sabotage that receive the most attention—women's self-sabotage, while quiet in form and hurtful only to the woman herself, is equally lethal. Passive forms of self-sabotage, the type women seem to be prone to, are harder to detect.

When a woman destroys her career because of self-demeaning thoughts and depressed behavior, it is just as much of a loss, if not as vivid, as when a man loses everything because of bankruptcy. Perhaps in the long run, self-demeaning thoughts are even more destructive to your career and self-image than financial mismanagement. Chronic illness is another way that women hurt themselves. This may not at first appear to be a form of self-sabotage, but unconsciously many women have sought medical help rather than fight for love or success. Probably as a result of this, women take more prescription drugs than men and become addicted to them more than men.

Janet is an example of a woman who sabotaged herself through illness. She had wanted to be married for as long as she could remember. When she met Chris, she thought her dreams had come true. As often happens, as their relationship became more serious, his difficulties surfaced. One problem with Chris was his son. Chris was forever fighting with his son because the boy needed money all the time. Chris always ended up giving him the money. Janet was upset about this, because one of the arguments Chris put forth against their getting a place together was money problems. Instead of telling him how angry and uncared for she felt, Janet became sick. She was tired, and she got every bug that went around. The doctors prescribed something new for every illness, but she was still exhausted.

Without realizing it, Janet was sabotaging herself with illness rather than expressing her feelings directly to Chris. Repressing these feelings, of course, was not good for her, nor for the relationship, which ended when Chris grew impatient with Janet for being sick all the time. The relationship might have ended anyway, but Janet would have felt stronger physically and emotionally had she expressed what she felt and explained what she wanted. Silent forms of self-sabotage, like Janet's illnesses, are ladylike, nonconfrontational, and don't make enemies for you. You wind up fighting yourself, not others.

Chris is obviously sabotaging this relationship even more than Janet, and he is losing out also. This is often true in romantic relationships. The man involved destroys what he's created for himself and his lover. In your career and in the rest of your life you will come up against men and women who unconsciously are out to defeat you. Keeping an eye out for these co-saboteurs is a skill you might well cultivate. Where you may encounter these people and how you can protect yourself is discussed in a later chapter. All of the efforts you exert to understand the causes and forms of your own sabotage will help you in dealing with these people.

It is an alarming fact of the last twenty years that women are increasingly using the same forms of self-sabotage that have gotten men much attention in the past. Just about as many women smoke now as men. The number of women smokers has increased, while the number of male smokers has decreased tremendously. And the number of women who drink alcohol has increased too. More than ever before, women admit that they're drinking more than they should. Whatever the causes for this are, and there are many, women are sabotaging themselves now in the same ways that men traditionally have. If you are in a relationship with a man or have been in one, you know that you most likely have helped him out with his problems more than he has helped you, and this includes his tendency to be self-destructive. This lopsided helpfulness may have begun with your father or brother; perhaps you are more concerned about your boss than he is about you. Whoever the man has been, you have watched over his potential for self-sabotage like a mother hen. Unfortunately no one has watched over you.

Jean witnessed a clear example of this. She shared a ski house with several men and women. One Saturday one of the older men spent several hours cutting wood for the fire. A few of the women tried to talk him into stopping because they were afraid he might injure himself. The next day the situation was reversed. Sarah, a somewhat older woman, tried cutting wood. Though Jean was concerned that Sarah also might overdo it, none of the men seemed to notice. Self-sabotage among women is not ordinarily as obvious as chopping too much wood too fast. As I have mentioned, it is most often quiet, internal, and hard for even a sensitive person to detect. But when you add to this the fact that men are generally less aware of emotional dynamics, you realize that you're going to have to be your own doctor, diagnosing and then healing your self-destructive tendencies.

On the brink of love or success, unconscious emotional

dragons can creep in to wreck the fulfillment that should rightfully be yours. After you have worked so hard for so long, once again things don't turn out right. In the following chapters, we will look at women who sabotaged themselves in different ways and how they triumphed in the end. We will then look at some of the deeper causes of self-sabotage, and at how you can fight co-saboteurs—whether lovers, relatives, or colleagues. Finally I'll offer a ten-point plan to help you stop sabotaging yourself. With this plan, you can become strong enough to slay your own dragons and win what you've always wanted, whether the struggle is with yourself or your boyfriend or your mother.

Rather than feel defeated and hopeless, you can have a sense of control and excitement about the possibilities of love and success that lie ahead for you. Remember, of course, to watch out for self-blame. Replace it with self-understanding, and give yourself much credit for having the honesty and openness to proceed through these chapters.

Part 1

THE FIVE BATTLEGROUNDS OF SELF-SABOTAGE

Women Who Fought and Won

CHAPTER 2

▼▼▼

YOUR BODY
AND SELF-SABOTAGE

▲▲▲

*When Illness, Fatigue,
or Accidents Defeat You*

▼▼▼▼▼▼▼▼▼▼▼▼▼▼▼▼▼▼▼▼▼▼▼▼▼▼▼▼▼▼▼▼

*My mother buried her anger against my father and I saw the effects
in her of this restraint—migraine headaches and tachycardia, to
name only two. The nervous system is very mysterious.*
—**May Sarton**

ILLNESSES are surely caused by germs, hereditary factors,
and drinking contaminated water, but they are also just as
surely caused by unconscious feelings, separations from
close family or friends, or unmet emotional needs. In 1917
Georg Groddeck, an eminent German psychoanalyst, pro-
posed that "Every person possesses this ability [to make
himself sick for whatever purposes] and everyone uses it
to a much greater extent than one can imagine." Yet when
I first suggest that we look at psychological reasons for
illness, my patients blame themselves for being sick. It is
easy to do this; I have fallen into the trap of self-blame as
well. If you have the courage to decide to examine the
emotional reasons you sabotage your body through recur-

ring illness or accidents, do not blame yourself, because self-blame can make you feel even sicker in the process. Remind yourself that there are psychological causes for every illness, and that those who become skillful at detecting their emotional reasons *without blaming themselves* are a step ahead with this vitally useful information. Always, of course, seek out the best in medical treatment as well. To understand how illnesses and emotions are connected, let's look at Gail's story.

GAIL

Single and in her late thirties, Gail was a science teacher at one of the top high schools in the city. Her sharp sense of humor and inquiring mind had made her well respected and popular among the students. Gail was attractive, with auburn hair and thoughtful hazel eyes. Yet if you looked further, you'd realize how exhausted she was most of the time. She seemed always to look as if she were about to come down with a virus. In fact, Gail spent a third of every school year out of work because of illness. Much of it had to be unpaid leave time; bills mounted up and she got into debt. She had never been a sickly child, so she was shocked that her body had let her down in her adult years.

Two years after she graduated from college she contracted hepatitis. This happened in the midst of a painful breakup with her college boyfriend, who decided he wanted to date other women. She was ill for several months and returned to live with her parents for a while. Eventually she got better, but Gail never really felt the same physically after that. She was susceptible to anything that went around, but it was the fatigue, low fevers, and overall body aches that kept her out of school. Often she was worse before menstruation. With a few days' rest she would improve—until the next episode. Each doctor Gail went to found something else to be the cause and prescribed a cure. Diagnoses of thyroid problem, allergies, anemia, and hypoglycemia had been made over the years, and each time Gail had taken the medication prescribed or changed her diet. For a while she felt some improvement, but the symptoms never really went away, and the debilitating tiredness and aching soon returned. Even on those days when she worked, she often came home and got straight into bed to recover for the next day. Gail drove herself crazy thinking that she was a hypochondriac and that she was making up her symptoms, but after she met other women who had similar problems, she felt less odd.

Gail is certainly not alone. Women visit medical doctors more often than men do, and more than half of all prescription medication goes to women. Some might use this information to prove that we are the "weaker" sex physically, but in reality we are the overworked sex. The fact that women go to doctors more often shows that most women are probably overburdened. But as in Gail's case, and equally important, we have no outlets for our strong emotions. These feelings can't be expressed any way but physically. This does not mean, however, that because Gail is in poor health she is not *really* sick, or that she is doing this to herself on purpose. Having observed myself when I am sick, as well as my patients, friends, and family, it appears that some illnesses occur because of emotional causes. This is true for men as much as for women. Gail does not want to be sick, but she is. Let's continue with her story.

When Gail felt better she became a different person. She was optimistic, loved to be busy, went out to theater and music events and race-walked for exercise. When she was well, Gail began courses toward the Ph.D. she wanted in psychological research. These courses were never completed, because illness always took over. Other projects, such as buying a summer cottage with some friends, were also dropped because of her health problems. The extra income she'd need would have to be earned either in a part-time job or during her free summers. How could she do that when she barely made it to the one job she already had?

Gail was the kind of woman who could never say no to anyone, whether she was asked for a favor or invited to socialize. As a result of being sick, though, Gail did slow down and say no to friends and family. She had always been protective of her mother and had special trouble saying no to her, as if the roles were reversed and Gail was the mother. No one else in the family had had health problems, except for her grandfather on her father's side, whom she was told had died young. Gail's parents were German and had lost many relatives in the war. Their depression and guilt about this pervaded the household, creating a quiet and depressed atmosphere.

Despite the fact that Gail was sick so much, she did meet men, and they were often attracted to her. Her last relationship ended because her boyfriend said he was tired of Gail's illnesses. He felt she could get better if she wanted to. Gail hated herself for a long while after that, but friends and a support group convinced her that he was as much to blame as her bad health. The man she had dated most recently, Howard, seemed to feel he could "cure" her and wanted them to live together, but Gail didn't feel she trusted him. She knew he couldn't cure her, no matter how much he cared. She also thought he wanted another child, but he already had a son that he could barely manage, since he tried to be a friend instead of a father to him. Gail felt that Howard wanted a woman because he didn't want the pressure of having to care for his son and make a home for them both. She knew she couldn't do this for him; she couldn't even take care of herself. She never said any of this out loud though. Each time they talked about their future, Gail felt physically worse the next day. She knew this was a losing situation for her and Howard, whether they moved in together or not.

How Gail Can Win Over Self-Sabotage

There are three basic steps that Gail can take to stop sabotaging her body, which we will examine in this section:

1. She can admit to herself that she wants and needs to be taken care of and find appropriate ways to have this occur without having to get sick.
2. She can speak up about her feelings and wishes, especially with her boyfriend. She can take the risk of asking for what she wants and saying no to what she does not want.
3. She can insist to herself that she has a right to have everything she wants in life, and she can refuse to play the family role of the sick one any longer.

Gail is obviously a very accomplished woman, with the potential to accomplish and achieve much more, both romantically and professionally. Yet she was unaware that one of the emotional reasons she got sick was because she wanted desperately to be taken care of, wanted others to show that they cared about her and about how she felt. This deep feeling was unacceptable to her conscious mind, just as it is unacceptable to many adults to admit this need, even though few of us received enough nurturance as children, and our daily schedules deplete us in any case. In Gail's family, you only got attention when you were sick. That was when her mother felt confident and took charge. The rest of the time Gail assumed the responsibility of bolstering her mother, making decisions for her but never getting credit. This role reversal depleted Gail more than she realized.

Nurturance is what Gail longed for, and as her unconscious mind understood this problem, sickness was her only hope of receiving it. She was most definitely ill when she was exhausted—her symptoms were certainly real. But her body was expressing more than a physical need. It was also saying, "I need to be taken care of."

If Gail was to accept her need to be nurtured, she could seek nurturance in different forms: from a therapist, friends, a boyfriend; possibly through more recognition in her work; through activities that fulfill her, such as exercise, massage, and creative outlets.

Gail automatically suppressed her feelings and needs in favor of other people. She didn't even realize she did this, relating to men and friends with complete confidence and making sure that others were happy and secure. Gail avoided telling other people what she really felt or wanted, as with Howard. She did not tell him that she could only live with him if he took full responsibility for his son. In order to improve her health, she must tell Howard that because he acts like a friend rather than a father to his son, she feels angry and scared. She was afraid that she would end up being the disciplinarian if they lived together. She must insist that a housekeeper be essential to his plan, something she knows Howard will be angry about. She ought to ask him if he plans to stay with her if her health doesn't improve. His reassurance would help her feel calmer and more trusting. Gail could feel better physically if she did this with him and with others. The emotions festering inside her would be aired, and she would have a chance to get what she wants and needs.

Last, Gail has to convince herself that she has a right to have the success and love that would bring her fulfillment. She does not naturally believe this because of the many opposite messages she heard growing up. Unconsciously, Gail was told to play the role of the "sick" one. Her father was used to having a sick person around, because his father had been ill when he was a child. But more important, as long as Gail was sick there would never be another man who could replace her father in her life. Gail unknowingly obeyed these unconscious messages and became the unhealthy one.

Because Gail's family lost many relatives in the war, they had a strong sense of guilt because they survived. Gail felt guilty also, and being sick was one way of expressing it, both for herself and the whole family. "We have our trials too—look at how sick poor Gail gets" might express how they felt. Once Gail begins to feel angry or even outraged about the unfairness of these veiled demands on her, the energy from this anger would help her battle her physical symptoms when they come upon her. Anger would help to wash away the guilt she carries around as well.

Gail needs to take control over her future away from her family. She could lead herself out of this family role if she told herself that she had a right to feel healthy and have what she wants, just like other people do, no matter what messages she intuitively received at home. Medical, nutritional, physical therapy, and exercise experts are all necessary to help Gail in her struggle. But Gail needs to find another source of nurturance, such as a therapist or group, to fill the void left by her inadequate parents so that she can be emotionally taken care of without having to sabotage herself through sickness.

The Beginning of a Healthier Future

Fortunately, Gail did work hard to stop sabotaging her body. She acknowledged that there were emotional causes for her illnesses, the most important one being that she wanted unconsciously to be taken care of by everyone she knew. She looked for ways to take better care of herself, scheduling weekly massage appointments and asking friends to listen to her problems as much as she listened to theirs. A nutritionist helped her construct a diet and vitamin regime that helped increase her energy. Slowly she is feeling better.

Gail told Howard what troubled her and what he would have to do for their relationship to work. He was at first angry and even refused to talk to her for a few days. Yet when she did finally see him with his son, Howard acted more like a responsible father. He also agreed that a house-keeper could take charge of his child if they lived together. As a result, they are considering living together for a trial period. Gail has felt better physically since she realized that she was annoyed at Howard and told him about it. She continues to feel weak around her family, but she is more and more aware of how her family contributed to her being sick. When she can feel angry about this, she notices that her aches and fever decrease. Gail has found a therapist who is helping her to fight emotionally for the life and the good health she wants.

Stress, Success, and Illness

Stress is one of the reasons that intelligent and capable women become ill. Sometimes the cause of the stress may be obvious, sometimes it is hidden. Stress is caused by too many responsibilities, but it also occurs because of feelings that have no outlet. Hans Selye, in his book *The Stress of Life*, explained that emotional states such as depression and disappointment can exhaust the adrenal gland so much that it is no longer able to produce the hormones your body needs to fight illness. Depression and disappointment can appear, surprisingly, when you are on the brink of love or success, or on your way to achieving either. Marilyn's case illustrates this.

MARILYN

In the last year, Marilyn turned thirty-four and changed from a smiling woman with an open face into someone who looked as if she'd been scared by a ghost. She was stunned by the misfortunes that seemed to have fallen on her from out of the sky, just as she was planning a wedding and getting recognition in her career.

Marilyn was a designer in the furniture department of a large department store chain. She planned the room displays from top to bottom. She had long felt very constrained working there, because her bosses were competitive to the point of being insulting. She used her engaging manner to handle them, but she'd swallowed a lot of anger during her ten years at the firm. As a way out, Marilyn developed her own small freelance interior design business, which had slowly been growing.

For five years, Marilyn had been going with Jim. She said this was the "most difficult but most passionate" relationship she'd ever had. Jim had an explosive temper, a demanding ex-wife, and children with an array of problems. In the first few years, Jim was late most of the time or canceled their plans at the last minute. When he was angry he was too often nasty, even abusive. He threatened to end the relationship so often that Marilyn learned to ignore what he said. But Marilyn worked hard on Jim, and his acting out and emotional explosions diminished.

Since the way Jim treated Marilyn had improved, they both thought about marriage. They'd been living together, with Jim subletting his apartment, but Jim said he never wanted to get married again and Marilyn didn't insist on it because of his many problems. Now, however, their marriage plans were definite, and Jim was even considering having the child that Marilyn wanted. Marilyn was ecstatic and felt safer with him than ever before.

There were also exciting changes in Marilyn's career. She was introduced to a groups of wealthy clients who thought she was great. One of these clients arranged for her to participate in a prestigious show of decorators. This was an absolute invitation to success, and Marilyn left her job at the store. She had to work harder than she'd ever worked in her life to get her "room" ready for the show. The show was a huge success, resulting in many new customers and many compliments for Marilyn. The day after the show ended, however, as she drove to see her mother, Marilyn was so exhausted that she dozed off and crashed into a street sign. She suffered whiplash and a bruised back that required her to stay in bed for the next month. She was terrified; if she had been driving faster, she might have been killed. Even though she resolved to take it easier, three weeks later Marilyn was back at work with renewed dedication. She had her new clients and a wedding to plan.

She and Jim decided to get married in four months. Marilyn was preoccupied with the arrangements and barely remembered to go for a gynecological checkup. When the doctor discussed the examination with her, she was stunned. He had found a small lump in her breast and wanted her to see a surgeon for an opinion about what it might be. Dazed, Marilyn went through the next few weeks of tests, surgery, and then the diagnosis. The lump was removed. It was cancerous but very small, self-contained and not of a dangerous form of malignancy. She did not have to have a mastectomy, but she did have some follow-up treatment. The prognosis was excellent.

But Marilyn was in a panic about this newest disaster. She wanted to postpone or even call off the wedding. She felt jinxed by the accident and the tumor and was terrified that some other terrible thing would happen to her body if she got married. Jim was evidently scared too; he said it was up to her to decide.

* * *

Dr. Louis Ormont, a well-known analyst, has said, "If there is no outlet for aggression, people can turn it against themselves, which raises further havoc with the way the body functions." He goes on to say that the physical symptoms that result can be anything "from a canker to a cancer." It can be frightening to realize that buried anger and other feelings, among other factors, can have so much influence on our physical health. But in Marilyn's situation, knowing this can in fact help her get some control over her body, *as long as she doesn't blame herself*, and as long as she realizes that her hidden emotional life is only one influence among many affecting whether or not she stays well. Nutrition, exercise, and inherited tendencies are among the many other factors. Let's see what Marilyn can do to stop sabotaging her body.

How Marilyn Can Win Over Self-Sabotage

Marilyn can have her marriage and her career and conquer self-sabotage of her body as long as she is vigilant in several areas. Of course she must investigate and utilize any possible medical, nutritional, and alternative treatments that could prevent a reoccurrence of her illness. The following suggestions, however, deal with the emotional measures she can take to defeat self-sabotage.

1. She can learn to understand fully how family messages have helped to create this problem within her.
2. She can give herself permission to be totally aware of all her deeper feelings, no matter how unpleasant they may be. She can find a support system such as group therapy to help her with this.
3. She can be extremely cautious physically whenever any good fortune occurs in her life, because this is a dangerous time for her.

4. She can learn to use visual imagery to help her battle illness and accidents.

Elmer and Alyce Green, who practice at the Menninger Clinic, state in their book *Beyond Biofeedback* that "every change in the mental emotional state, conscious or unconscious, is accompanied by an appropriate change in the physiological state." Every good thing that happens to Marilyn causes an emotional change deep inside, hidden even from her. And each emotional change, because it is suppressed, causes a physical change.

Until now, Marilyn has been busy being good and responsible and working hard, like so many women. She doesn't take time to think about her own feelings. But once she knows what these are, a tremendous pressure on her body will be released. Her conflicting feelings about love and success have built up so much that they can't be expressed except through illness (or an accident). These very strong conflicts about marriage and success activate what are inherited "weak links" in her physical makeup that make her susceptible to particular physical problems. Here are the messages her family unconsciously conveyed to her, through their behavior and their own illnesses, and the feelings that are suppressed, which in part have caused her to sabotage her body.

Q "You should express anxiety, anger, fear, and resentment through physical symptoms, not out loud."

Marilyn's father's had chronic back problems, which came and went apparently without cause. He never at any time expressed authentic feelings. The family silently knew, however, that when he was sick his illness conveyed his real feelings. He was resentful about taking care of them but did not admit this to himself. He wanted and needed to be taken care of but could not admit this either. When he went to bed with his bad back, he got the care he wanted.

Marilyn understandably is overwhelmed with feelings about all of her new situations. The only way to escape being trapped on the same work treadmill she saw her father on is to do what he did—get put in bed with a bad back.

Q "Mother gets sick when she is abandoned. You should not get married because she will feel abandoned."

Marilyn's parents were divorced when she was a teenager. Her mother insisted that she was glad Dad called it quits because she had complained about him from the day they married, but in reality she felt abandoned by him. When they divorced, she developed breast cancer—her unconscious method of being taken care of when she felt alone. She was actually furious and hurt that Marilyn's father left, even though she said she wanted this. Marilyn devoted herself to her mother while her mother was sick and pulled her through. On one level Marilyn understands that the tie between herself and her mother will be different after the marriage, and she is unconsciously afraid that her mother might get sick again. More important, though, is that Marilyn will feel terribly separate and alone being married. These hidden separation fears that are building up before the wedding precipitate the onset of cancer to which she is predisposed.

Q "In our family, we can't keep love alive in a marriage. And we don't fulfill ourselves creatively or financially."

Marilyn learned this from the bad marriage and divorce of her parents, and by seeing them creatively unfulfilled for years. She is fearful that her marriage will be as bad as the one she saw at home, that she has "inherited" the inability to keep love in her life, that her creative talent as a decorator is just a flash in the pan and will soon disappear. All these fears are expressed through illness and accidents as she tries to unconsciously sabotage what she has worked for because she fears it will disappear anyway.

* * *

In 1966, the analyst L. LeShan wrote, "One condition predisposing to cancer was an inability to use aggression as a self-protective tool. Envy, jealousy, competition, and resentment are squelched." All of these feelings have been squelched in Marilyn's family, as they are in many families. But this family is predisposed to bodily injury. Being aware of the messages and feelings will help to build a strong protective wall between illness, accidents, and Marilyn.

Marilyn must also forever be aware that especially good events in her life may cause her to sabotage herself. If she keeps herself on the alert for this (she might even pin a note on her refrigerator: BE CAREFUL WHEN LIFE IS GOING TOO WELL), she will have a better chance to get what she wants and remain healthy. Being on the alert means taking care of her health even more than usual, and taking special care to avoid accidents when everything seems rosy.

Visual imagery, also called visualization, is a technique that is often used to combat illness. I will describe it in detail, with specific steps for developing your own particular images, in the last chapter. Marilyn needs to use this technique to develop a "fighting attitude," so that she can keep what she's worked for. She needs to visualize her life as a battle between her strong self and the forces and feelings that seek to sabotage her, as well as a battle between good health and illness. The images should always place her in the winning position. She can use these images and phrases to strengthen her during dangerous periods.

Marilyn on the Road to a Safer Life

Following the above steps was not easy for Marilyn, but she married and her business is expanding. A therapy group is helping her understand how her husband, her family, and her work influence her. The therapy ensures that her feelings don't stay bottled up. She has had another minor car accident—no physical injuries this time—and the flu last year almost became pneumonia. But neither was a life-threatening problem, in part because she was aware enough to watch out for danger and to use her visual images. Most important, Marilyn does not push down her feelings and try to be happy all the time, although others may think that she has it all. Often she feels sad or angry. She has learned to live with the mixture of feelings that is really her essential self. She no longer feels as young and innocent as she once did, but she has more confidence that she'll live to a ripe old age.

A SELF-HELP TEST—ARE YOU SABOTAGING YOUR BODY?

These brief questions will help you decide *without self-blame* if this is your form of self-sabotage. If you answer yes to any of the following questions, you are very likely on the way to sabotaging your body. Remember, it is never too late to change a pattern of self-sabotage. Use any of the steps suggested in this chapter or in the final chapter.

1. Are you ill so much that it gets in the way of meeting men or having a long-term relationship?
2. Have accidents ever occurred at a time when you were just about to get something you wanted?
3. Do infections or illness keep you from having sex or prevent you from enjoying sex?
4. If you're with someone now, have you had recurring illnesses or chronic fatigue since the relationship started?
5. If you're single now, have you been ill more often than usual since your last relationship ended?
6. Have you had so much trouble with recurring illness or accidents that you have been unable to work or unable to succeed as you wished?

7. Have you ignored warnings that you are damaging or neglecting your health? Do you secretly fantasize that one day you will become seriously ill or have a serious accident?

▼▼▼▼▼▼▼▼▼▼▼▼▼▼▼▼▼▼▼▼▼▼▼▼▼▼▼▼▼

CHAPTER 3

LOVE
AND
SELF-SABOTAGE

▲▲▲▲▲▲▲▲▲▲▲▲▲▲▲▲▲▲▲▲▲▲▲▲▲▲▲▲▲▲

And most of all would I flee from the cruel madness of love.
—Alfred, Lord Tennyson

ALL of us at some time have experienced Tennyson's cruel madness of love. Yet for certain women love is always unrelentingly cruel, even though these same women are winners in life's other arenas. These are the women who sabotage themselves only in their relationships with men, while their careers move steadily onward, friends are as plentiful as they want, and they get pleasure out of a wide variety of exciting interests. When it comes to men, the dream of having it all ends; a fulfilling, committed, secure, and loving relationship is always out of reach. And self-sabotage is, at least in part, the cause.

You are not to blame if love is your area of self-sabotage.

Blaming yourself will hinder rather than help you. You are not bad or wrong or stupid when you do what you do. You are not wrong if your pattern is to find men who reject or even mistreat you. And you are not bad if you reject the "nice" guy or are mean to a man who's good to you. There are reasons, often unconscious ones, for everything you do. We will look at some of these reasons in this chapter. But remember that men sabotage relationships even more than women and will often try to undermine efforts to make things better. You can find help for this problem in the chapter in the latter part of this book which tells you how to cope with the "co-saboteurs," lovers and others who try to keep you from getting what you want.

If happiness in love is what you want, it is first essential that you become aware of all your deeper feelings and conflicts. Your willingness to evaluate yourself means that you are stronger than most and more likely to overcome whatever old patterns are binding you, just as many of my patients have done over the years. Roberta's pattern of becoming involved with men who reject her is a common one.

ROBERTA

Tall, with vivid blue eyes, Roberta at twenty-nine was a vibrant woman who reached out to everyone she met. No one suspected that she ever got depressed—until the topic came around to men. Roberta wanted to be married or at least to come home each day to a man she loved, but this had never happened to her. She wondered if this was a family problem, since her brother couldn't maintain a relationship either. He broke up with women one right after the other. Roberta had the opposite problem. She never broke up with anyone. Men broke up with her.

Roberta went over and over in her mind what she might have done wrong, but the end result was the same. Men ultimately rejected her, whether they were nice about it, like Dick, who bought her flowers every week and then disappeared, or awful, like Matt, who always waited to the last minute to ask her out and turned out to be married after all. Rejection was inevitable. Like clockwork, Roberta would go out on three or four dates with a man; then he wouldn't call again. Of the dozen men that she had dated in two years, this happened with each one. They seemed nice, but they always turned out to be creeps. Occasionally Roberta stopped dating, which made her feel hopeless, bored, and lonely. A few months of this and she was back into the dating scene again.

Roberta was a manager in a telecommunications firm and supervised a staff of five. She had been teaching herself about the latest developments in the field and was asked to go with a delegation to Washington to attend a conference on satellite communications. There were other exciting areas of her life as well. One of her dreams was to play the flute with a jazz group, and recently her teacher had brought her together with some other musicians. Their band was beginning to happen, and Roberta was in heaven. Exercising, seeing her friends—her life was busy and satisfying. She even finally decorated her apartment, rather than waiting to do it with the right man. But Roberta *was* waiting for the right man, and she was feeling more and more frustrated.

Roberta thought that perhaps all the better men were married already, like her boss. She'd been flirting with him for years, although she never did anything about it. But sometimes it seemed that if it wasn't for his flattering attention, Roberta would have to think men ran the way they did because something was wrong with her.

How Roberta Can Win in Love

If rejecting men wore signs saying, as Shakespeare put it, "I pray you do not fall in love with me, For I am falser than vows made in wine," women like Roberta would not get rejected and hurt. But men don't wear signs and Roberta did get hurt, because she was blind to the negative qualities of the men she dated and equally blind to the good qualities of men she might have dated. There are four steps Roberta can take to win over self-sabotage:

> **1.** She can convince herself that she has a right to be who she really is with a man, that she can keep her music and her career even if she should find a long-term relationship.
> **2.** She can start to believe that she is a terrific woman and that her emotions, including her anger, are an asset that can help her in her relationships.
> **3.** She can come to realize that she does not have to keep her parents together, and that she must take the risk of emotionally separating from them.
> **4.** She can recognize that her feelings for her boss are deeper than she realizes and are stopping her from taking other men seriously.

Roberta has a right to be who she really is with a man. She has been afraid that she might lose her independence, her creativity in her music and her job, the success she has managed strenuously to nurture and its rewards. Her "self" that has accomplished all this felt fragile, as if when the right man came along, she could be squashed flat as easily as an ant. Roberta did not realize that she was afraid of losing herself to a man. She didn't recognize that as soon as she met a man, she began to give up parts of her personality. For example, if a man wanted to get together on a night her music group was meeting, she would skip her evening of music. Roberta must first become aware of her tendency to give up her separateness and then observe how she does this and how scared it makes her deep inside.

Roberta must start to believe that she is terrific and that her emotions are an asset. Unconsciously, Roberta has also been afraid that were she to live with a man, he would discover the "real" her—a "bitch," a terribly pushy woman—and he would leave her. She thought she was far too impatient too often. A man would only stay with her if she was perfect, or so her parents had told her. They also told her in many indirect ways that she was not nice, that she was nasty and angry and "impossible to live with." In reality, Roberta is a lovely woman whose sensitivity, including her anger, would be a tremendous asset in a romantic relationship. Once she feels proud of her feelings and has confidence in who she is emotionally, it is much less likely that men she likes will reject her.

Roberta must separate emotionally from her parents. Mom and Dad have been a strong barrier between Roberta and any man. They live nearby and have been intertwined in her life. Roberta has had to call her mother after every date, or she feels anxious and guilty. The phone calls are close and warm, especially when she has been rejected again by a man. Roberta understands how much Mom and Dad need her in order to be happy. She knows that she kept their marriage calm, and she remembers how badly they seemed to get along when she went away to college for one year. She remembers how cold they were to each other, and the tension she felt. One summer Mom and Dad even separated for a month. Roberta hated seeing her parents each so alone, and unconsciously she would sacrifice her love life to prevent this from happening again.

Roberta needs to believe that she is not responsible for her parents' relationship. One step she can take to help her separate from them is to stop calling her mother so frequently and to stop discussing men with her. This action may make her feel very anxious, and she will need support to keep her resolve.

Roberta must also recognize that her feelings for her boss are sabotaging her. She fantasizes about being married to her boss more than she admits. He is an authority figure to her and is very charming—far more charming than he is as a husband. Roberta's boss needs her admiration even more than she needs him, and she has been raised, as we can see, to give other people what they need. Deep down, she is also scared that he might be depressed if she were to fall in love. The most important thing Roberta can do, however, is to understand that she has stronger feelings about her boss than she acknowledges, and that these are causing a block that prevents her from having a real relationship.

Roberta Moves Closer to Love

Perhaps because Roberta is nearing thirty, she decided to take her problem with men more seriously. She has tried out various support groups and is listening to the advice of good friends and accepting the nurturance of the groups. Roberta is starting to believe that she is as nice a person as anyone else, and that her anger and impatience don't make her unfit for a relationship. The last time she met a new man, she resolved not to turn her schedule inside out for him. As a result, he seemed to treat her with more respect than others had, and has stayed around longer. She is no longer as eager to please. Roberta has been unable to cut down on her phone calls to her mother, but she has managed to steer the subject off of the men she dates, even though her mother seems annoyed. And Roberta now understands that her feelings for her boss keep her away from other men. Observing him more critically, she has begun to realize that he is not a man she would want to spend her life with even if he were free, although she still finds him very attractive. The man she's dating now may not turn out to be "the" man, but she thinks that this time she will be the one to decide whether to leave or stay.

Another all too common pattern is that of women who stick like glue to men who mistreat them.

URSULA

Ursula had been with Eddie for six years. She dated their relationship from the time she bought her house and needed an insurance agent, who turned out to be Eddie. She was thirty-five when she met him, and everything seemed to fall into place. But six years later her romance had turned into a nightmare from which she couldn't escape.

Ursula knew that she wanted a man in her life to complete her happiness, and Eddie seemed at first to be the one. They had a great sex life, and he was warm and sensitive and fun. But soon he began to mistreat her. Eddie had many women friends. He said that they meant nothing to him, but Ursula was sure he was lying. Too many times he was out all night, and a few times Ursula had proof that he lied about his alibi. When she was at his place women called and hung up when she answered his phone. Ursula tried to break up with Eddie because of the other women, but she couldn't stand to be away from him. All he had to do was swear that he had given up even having women as friends and she succumbed. Ursula tried to see other men, but no one excited her as much as Eddie.

Money was another problem between them, because Eddie never had any. He refused to say where his money went, and Ursula ended up paying for everything. Once she even considered hiring a private detective to find out about Eddie's money and his women. But she didn't really want to know, because she couldn't imagine her life without Eddie. Yet the pain caused by his secret "activities" wore her out emotionally, and physically as well. Ursula didn't know why she was glued to a man who caused her so much pain. Ursula had to give up her needs and feelings to keep the relationship together.

Ursula had slowly become well-known as the hostess of a popular local TV talk show. She had achieved recognition and awards for her provocative but empathetic and humorous interviewing style. The small house she bought just within the city limits allowed her to walk to work on nice days. Sometimes she felt that she had everything that she possibly wanted. Even restoring her house had been fun; seeing it emerge from the layers of paint and linoleum made the hours of work worthwhile and turned what could have been a job into a hobby. When she first met Eddie, he had been really enthusiastic and had pitched in, as if they might live there together someday. His enthusiasm for stripping paint or living together didn't last very long, though. There was no doubt Ursula was in charge of her show and her home, but she felt she had no control over the Eddie half of her life.

How Ursula Can Win Over Self-Sabotage

Despite her fame and success, Ursula didn't know how to take care of herself in the world of men, and she got glued to a man who mistreated her. It is possible, however, for her to overcome this form of self-sabotage by taking the following steps:

1. She must recognize that she is emotionally addicted to Eddie, but that in fact she can live without him.
2. She must show Eddie in actions and words that she will no longer rescue him from his problems. She must decide

that she deserves to be loved for who she is not what she does for someone else.

3. She must stop blaming herself for Eddie's problems.

4. She must realize that guilt from her past is keeping her with Eddie, that she confuses him with her father.

John Dryden could have been describing an addictive relationship when he wrote, "Pains of love be sweeter far, than all other pleasures are." Despite all the pleasures that Ursula has in her life, nothing she has accomplished or that anyone else does for her matters as much as Eddie. She is hooked on him, on the pain and the small pleasure he gives her.

A first step then is to realize that she is hooked on him and feels her life depends on him. Next she must convince herself that she will not die without him, although she feels that she will. She feels as if he is her parent and she is a helpless child, when in fact Eddie is the one who is barely able to manage.

"Pity me that the heart is slow to learn, What the swift mind beholds at every turn," wrote Edna St. Vincent Millay. In her mind Ursula knows that she should not tolerate being treated poorly by Eddie, but emotionally she feels desperate. Her heart is a slow learner. To grasp her real inner strengths, she should attend one of the many support groups that have sprung up for women in addictive relationships. Other people may help her see that she is extremely well equipped to live without Eddie. A support group will help her build the confidence she needs in order to find someone else if Eddie continues to mistreat her.

Ursula has taken care of Eddie, just as she took care of her family. She rescued him from his financial messes and went back to him even after he had been with other women, because unconsciously she knew he needed her even more than she needed him. She hated to think that he might suffer. If Ursula can tell Eddie that she will no longer bail him out every time he needs money, and if she will stick to her decision he will be forced to improve his financial situation. He might, of course, look for another woman who will give him money. If that occurs, Ursula will then know that he was only using her for her money and she was wise to rid herself of him. Eddie will never change if Ursula continues to give him money.

Similarly, his affairs with other women will continue until Ursula takes a stand or threatens to end the relationship. She could also insist that they try couples therapy. All of these actions are risky but necessary if she wants to have a better relationship, with him or with someone else. Ursula blamed herself when Eddie flirted with other women and had affairs. She thought she was not attractive anyway, and this just confirmed it. (Actually she's very striking.)

Ursula needs to change the negative thinking about herself that she originally learned at home and that Eddie's behavior causes her to perpetuate. But Ursula must understand that Eddie has serious problems of his own, which developed long before he met her, and that he would act like this with any woman. She can repeat to herself, "Eddie has affairs because of his own personal problems. It has nothing to do with me. I am an attractive woman and deserve better."

It's also important for Ursula to recognize that Eddie is not her father and that she should not feel guilty about her past. Ursula came from an abusive background, which has kept her connected to Eddie. Her parents fought all the time, and when she was ten her father began to molest her. Too scared to talk about it, she hid this from her mother for a year, until finally it came out in an emotional outburst.

Mom had long wanted a reason to leave Dad and so quickly left with the children.

Because her father acted on his sexual feelings toward Ursula, she unconsciously duplicated her childhood by staying with Eddie, a man who is not faithful and acts on his sexual feelings toward other women. But Ursula can remind herself that Eddie is not her father, and that she has choices now she did not have as a child. She does not have to stay with him, as she had to stay with her father. She can also remind herself that she is a strong adult woman now who can take a stand in favor of monogamy. Guilt also plays a role for Ursula. Women who have been molested by their fathers often are unjustly burdened with guilt. They feel they are "bad" just as children from divorced families often feel guilty. Both situations existed for Ursula and contribute to her underlying guilt. She can utilize therapy and support groups to help her realize that in fact she has no reason to feel guilty and that she does deserve more from love.

Slowly Leaving Eddie

Glued to Eddie for years, it has been slow and difficult for Ursula to break away from him. But she has made progress. She stopped giving Eddie money, and he did not leave her. With the help of a therapist, Ursula understands now that she confuses Eddie with her father. She was able to insist that he stop seeing other women. When he continued to have affairs, Ursula broke up with him, but she was only able to remain away from him for two months. Yet that is the longest period she has been able to detach herself from him in six years, and she gave herself credit for that. She has also begun to date other men for the first time in years, although she is still seeing Eddie. Though none of these men has clicked for her so far, she's trying to learn not to blame herself when Eddie or any other man has problems that interfere with a relationship.

* * *

Sometimes a woman will sabotage a relationship just as she achieves success. This was Vanessa's problem.

VANESSA

Vanessa had been married to Gregory for ten years when she left him. They met when they were in their mid-twenties and both were social workers at a family service clinic. They instantly became best friends and lovers. Later they went to the same university, each earning a master's degree in social work. When Gregory decided to become a therapist and began attending an analytic training institute, Vanessa did the same. Eventually they were married. During these ten years, no two people could have been closer. Their friends and parents thought of Vanessa and Gregory as the perfect couple.

When they had been married eight years, Jane, a mutual friend, came to Vanessa and Gregory with an idea about a health food center that would also offer weight-loss and nutritional counseling. She was looking for partners. For the first time since they had met, Vanessa and Gregory reacted differently. Vanessa was thrilled and excited by the prospect; Gregory was not. But he encouraged Vanessa to join Jane in this venture anyway.

Starting with a small storefront and one diet group, the business soon expanded. Vanessa's training in social work made it easy for her to fall right into this sort of counseling, and Jane was a natural in the business and selling end. They moved to a bigger store and started thinking about starting a second center. Gregory and Vanessa spent less time together now than at any time during their marriage. Vanessa worked many evenings, and gave lectures and attended conferences. She was having fun and feeling independent for the first time in her life!

Gregory soon felt abandoned. He complained that Vanessa never made dinner anymore, never even came home for dinner. The more he said this, the angrier Vanessa got. She told him to make his own dinners, she wasn't there to take care of him. His reaction would be to mope at home and wait for her arrival, no matter how late it was. Vanessa felt repulsed by his behavior and found she was no longer attracted to him sexually. She went along with his frequent sexual overtures to appease him. He was immature, she felt. He had never been in the business world.

Vanessa thought about breaking up their marriage, but she was scared to be alone. She met an interesting and charming man at a conference and later saw him for lunch. Eventually they slept together. Vanessa felt guilty, but she was even more repulsed by Gregory. Finally she left him. Once Vanessa was established in her own place, however, she felt panicky. She wanted what Gregory wanted, a home and children. What had happened? The new man had begun to pull away from her as soon as she told him she was separating from her husband. She still saw Gregory, but he might start dating. What if he met someone else? Vanessa didn't know what had come over her to make her move out so impulsively after ten years of marriage.

Meanwhile, as usual, her parents and older brother had been haranguing her to move back home and not to live alone. They treated her the same way at thirty-four as they had when she was twelve. She had only managed to get away from them the first time because of Gregory.

How Vanessa Can Win Over Self-Sabotage

"Whatever you do," said Voltaire, "stamp out abuses, and love those who love you." This is excellent advice for

Vanessa to follow, but she doesn't. Instead of trying to stamp out what she dislikes about her marriage and continuing to love the man who loves and wants to be with her, on the brink of success, she sabotages herself and runs from her problems for many reasons, past and present. But Vanessa can have it all—her work and Gregory. These are the steps she should follow.

> 1. She should learn to understand that she can be furious with her husband and still stay with him. She needs to learn to accept and express her feelings.
> 2. She must be willing to work on the relationship and ask for what she wants.
> 3. She should learn to recognize how childhood power struggles affect her relationships today.
> 4. She should allow herself to be close to many people at once. She does not have to choose between her business partner and her husband.

Vanessa and Gregory are experiencing very real conflicts that most couples face when one partner changes after they have been close for many years. Vanessa wants to grow as a separate person from Gregory, and he is generally encouraging of this, but he is scared that he will lose her. He regresses, becomes a little boy. Vanessa could try to be understanding—she would be scared if Gregory had gone off on a new venture. She could reassure him that he won't lose her and make sure to have dinner with him a few nights a week.

But Vanessa does not want to do this because she has so much anger that is not expressed. She thinks her anger is bad and thus holds it in. She's afraid that a man would leave her if she expressed anger in front of him. Instead she expresses her anger through overwork and an affair. Gregory shows his anger by sulking. Both have to accept their negative feelings and express them. They must realize that the only way to save their marriage is to agree that they need a new relationship, one where anger and differences are permitted. Their old relationship has become too confining for them. Anger does not have to terminate the relationship, it can actually improve it.

Improving a relationship takes hard work. Too frequently women and men sabotage their long-standing love life because of success, instead of giving as much time and attention to improving the relationship as they do to their work. Many relationships, like Vanessa and Gregory's marriage, can be saved. It is always best not to break up a relationship when your career is zooming skyward, but rather to seek counseling and give yourself some adjustment time. Wait until the growth spurt is over and assess your feelings then.

If Vanessa realizes this, she might decide to work on the marriage. She and Gregory need a place, such as in marital therapy, to express their feelings safely, rather than letting them build up to explode in impulsive acts. Working on the marriage does not mean that Vanessa has to give up her new self. She needs to learn to say what she wants, have her new life, and still be able to enjoy her marriage. Vanessa will have to take the first steps toward improving their marriage, since generally men do not initiate change, but Gregory will most likely respond to suggestions from her.

In order to work to improve her marriage, Vanessa must recognize how her childhood affects her relationship. In Vanessa's family, she was smothered by her mother each time she attempted to be independent. Her mother was delighted when Vanessa married Gregory, because she did not want Vanessa to live alone. She tried to get Vanessa to move back home when she left him. Her father always remained neutral.

Some of the anger Vanessa feels toward Gregory is confused with her anger toward her mother for controlling her and toward her father for his passivity. She feels Gregory is trying to control her too, but he is actually much more supportive than her mother ever was. Vanessa does not have to "leave home" to assert herself with Gregory. Yet unconsciously she feels as powerless as she did with her mother; she feels she has no alternative but to leave Gregory impulsively. It will help Vanessa to recognize that the power struggle and anger are as much with her parents as they are with Gregory.

Once in her own business, Vanessa feels closer to her partner, Jane, than to her husband. The closer she is to Jane, the more she is repulsed by her husband. She is "splitting," a term psychotherapists use to describe the feeling you have that you can trust only one person (usually a parent) at a time. This condition is created by parents who, without realizing it, do not allow a child to feel anything negative toward them. The child's negative feelings may go toward the other parent or toward a sibling instead. The result for Vanessa is that she feels she cannot have her business partner and her husband—success and love—at the same time. She acted the same way when she was first married: she stayed close to her husband and excluded all others. Vanessa needs to change this habit, and Gregory must learn to expand his friendships also.

Love and Success for Vanessa

Vanessa did decide to return to Gregory to work on their marriage, on a month-to-month basis. So far she's still there. They have dinner together two or three nights a week, and Gregory has stopped sulking as much, even though Vanessa works a lot. Vanessa continues to feel angry at him, but more often she's telling him what makes her angry. Sometimes he will get angry too, and sometimes he does go into a sulk. His sulks still provoke her so much that sometimes she even leaves for a while. She can now see, though, that when Gregory does this it reminds her of her father. Recently Vanessa is thinking of having a child, and this is bringing them closer again.

A SELF-EVALUATION TEST—ARE YOU SABOTAGING YOUR LOVE LIFE?

If you answer yes to any one of the following questions, you may be sabotaging your love life in the particular way indicated. Don't blame yourself. Make sure to read the chapter on co-saboteurs so that you'll also recognize it when men are sabotaging you. Then use the steps suggested here and in the final chapter to help you to slowly but surely do what others have done—fight self-sabotage and achieve the relationship you want with a man.

For Single Women (women not involved in a monogamous relationship)

1. Do you put off meeting available men because you feel committed to a man who is married or who sees other women in addition to you?

2. In the past two years, have you had more than one affair with a married man?

3. Do you use work or family as an excuse for not taking the time to meet men?

4. Do you give up your independence, career, sense of self when you are seeing a man?

5. If a man rejects you, do you remain obsessed with him, refusing to meet other men because you are waiting for him to return?

6. Do you take any type of rejection by a man as an indication that you are unlovable or unattractive or uninteresting?

7. Do you take care of any man you date, from the first phone call on, helping him with his problems but never evaluating what you are getting in return? When it ends, do you feel used?

8. Have you been rejected by every man you've dated in the past year or two?

For the Woman Who Is Married or Involved in a Monogamous Relationship

1. Do you simmer and burn but never bring up the real problems?

2. Do you blame yourself every time there's a disagreement?

3. Do you just want to get out of the relationship without making any attempt to resolve the problems?

4. If your sex life is a problem, do you are ignore this?

5. Do you imagine finding a perfect man and a relationship with no problems at all? Are you having an affair now or are you considering having one as a way of avoiding the real issues?

6. If your partner is having an affair, do you pretend not to notice or allow this to continue in some other way?

7. Do you feel that success is far more important than your relationship? Do you overwork to avoid dealing with your partner and your relationship?

8. Are you waiting for your partner to bring up problems or suggest counseling? (This rarely happens.)

CHAPTER 4

▼▼▼▼▼▼▼▼▼▼▼▼▼▼▼▼▼▼▼▼▼▼▼▼▼

COMPULSIONS

▲▲▲▲▲▲▲▲▲▲▲▲▲▲▲▲▲▲▲▲▲▲▲▲▲

The Habits That Sabotage You

▼▼▼▼▼▼▼▼▼▼▼▼▼▼▼▼▼▼▼▼▼▼▼▼▼▼▼▼▼▼▼▼▼▼▼▼▼

> *[She] that hath no rule over [her] own spirit is like a city that is*
> *broken down and without walls.*
> *—Taylor Caldwell*

THE dictionary defines a compulsion as an "irresistible urge." You may think of this kind of urge as an addiction. Whichever term you use, when you are hooked on alcohol, drugs, work, food, or even on being late, you do not "rule your own spirit." In the following case, Darla's spirit was ruled by her compulsions.

DARLA

Darla, a trim, sun-bleached-blonde, thirty-one-year-old graduate student, had traveled halfway around the world on underwater expeditions with a famous oceanographic research institute. She was one of only a handful of women to be involved in this type of research and study, and she loved her work. She learned to scuba dive alongside her father at ten and had rarely been out of the water since. (Both Darla's parents are scientists; her mother's an engineer, her father a biologist.) On an expedition in the Caribbean last summer, she actually identified an underwater plant species that was thought not to grow any longer in the region. The leader of the expedition was thrilled and encouraged her to write up the discovery for a prestigious journal. The article was accepted and published, an achievement that few graduate students can claim. Darla admitted that she was the "pet" of the expedition and basked in the glory.

At school, however, Darla did not find any glory. When she respected a professor, she worked hard and got along well. But in most classes, she felt contemptuous of what she thought was the low level of the course, and her contempt toward her professors showed. These teachers disliked her and made their courses harder for her. No one realized that deep down she was scared, and that in order to make it through school she was severely damaging her health.

Darla was hooked on caffeine and nicotine, especially when she was under pressure. As soon as she started to think about a paper or an exam coming up, her anxiety became unbearable, and she chain-smoked and drank coffee and diet cola in a robotlike fashion. Two packs of cigarettes and ten sodas or ten cups of coffee disappeared quickly. During the last "siege," as she called it when work was due, she smoked so much she developed a bad cough. The doctor said this was a smoker's cough and an early warning of more devastating problems to come unless she stopped. But Darla's attempts to stop or at least cut down were halfhearted, and her success rate reflected this. The more she cut down on cigarettes, the more diet cola and coffee she drank. Darla realized she was out of control. She got stomachaches from all the caffeine, felt jumpy all the time, and couldn't sleep.

Yet none of this was as bad as when Darla dropped all her bad habits. Then she felt lifeless and without energy. She said she couldn't concentrate on her work or function at all, and she felt that she had to. She had no choice but to keep going. Darla had one more habit: when she finished work for the day, she smoked marijuana to help her relax. She said her marijuana use was no problem, the same as having a martini after work. It was not connected to her other "habits," she felt.

Dr. John L. Falk says, "You are addicted when your use of something is excessive and causes negative social or medical consequences." Freud and others see the problem differently, however. They say that addiction is an effort to escape from stressful situations by doing something regressive that puts you in a state of "euphoria" or calm instead. You have a problem if you use this "thing" to avoid negative feelings on a regular basis. This is what Darla did.

It seemed like a contradiction, but Darla only liked men who didn't have any addiction problems themselves. She put herself on her best behavior and didn't smoke or drink coffee or use any marijuana in front of someone she was dating. Since she couldn't tolerate doing without for long, though, her relationships were limited, usually ending after several weeks of infatuation, before either person became their real self. When she was seeing a man, she sometimes felt like a kid again, spraying deodorant around her apartment to get rid of the cigarette odor before he arrived, as she used to do to hide the smell from her parents.

When Darla met a man who smoked or drank a lot or seemed addictive in any way, she had no respect for him.

Darla didn't realize that this meant that she also had little respect for herself. Her newest man was another non-smoker whom she wanted to see more frequently. But he hated cigarettes. She was scared to death that he would find out about all her habits. He had already asked her about her cough and raspy voice.

How Darla Can Win Over Self-Sabotage

Complex as Darla's problem may seem, a remedy to her habits can be found once she decides to give up her addictive behavior and learn to tolerate the feelings that emerge. What will not help her is to blame or criticize herself because she self-sabotages through addictions. This will only tie her in knots emotionally, causing her to want to abuse caffeine or smoke even more. Self-awareness and the resolve to take it one day at a time are the effective remedies. Darla should try the following steps to help her defeat self-sabotage, along with using a stop-smoking program and Narcotics Anonymous.

1. She should begin, taking it one day at a time, to experience her feelings rather than medicate them.
2. She should explore the ways her family, especially her father, is connected with her compulsive and addictive behavior.
3. She should realize that she does not have to be perfect to succeed.
4. She should learn to believe she can survive and do well without her "fixes."

Darla is a gifted and emotionally sensitive woman. Her sensitivity could be an attribute, but it has become a liability for her. Instead of experiencing her feelings and dealing with her anxieties about school, relationships, and success, she "medicates" herself with caffeine, nicotine, and drugs.

This "medication" soothes her anxiety and anger, but it is destructive and potentially physically disastrous in the long run.

In order to stop this form of self-sabotage, Darla must decide to quit one of her addictions. She might start with marijuana, with the support of a group organized to help people with this problem, such as Narcotics Anonymous. Darla will immediately experience many feelings that these substances were hiding. A group will help her with these feelings, so that she does not have to return to her fixes for help. As any of the Anonymous groups recommend, Darla should only promise herself she'll stay drug free "one day at a time," because long-range resolutions do not work.

Darla's connection to her father is very strong, for better or worse. Mom was closer to Darla's two younger sisters. Dad nurtured her mind and gave her a love of the ocean, but he also unconsciously taught her to deny her feelings through addictive behavior. Darla's father smoked until he developed emphysema. He has high blood pressure. He is a high-strung man who was terrified of his own feelings because he thought they would overwhelm him. When he was younger he took Valium to cope with his feelings, as well as smoking cigarettes.

As all children do, Darla looked to her parents to teach her how to deal with frustration and anxiety. She unconsciously does what she learned from her father. The unconscious message he conveyed to her was, "All feelings are scary. Feelings mean something terrible is about to take place. Do something"—take something—"and you will be all right." This vague feeling of doom immediately leads to a cigarette, coffee, or marijuana. Darla's mother, an engineer, was a role model as a career woman, but she was not a good model for Darla when it came to coping with feelings. Her mother was jealous of the closeness between her husband and Darla and let this stop her from being the mother her daughter needed. Darla felt that Mom didn't care about her.

Darla does not have to break away from her parents to stop sabotaging herself, but understanding where her problem comes from will help her to understand also that it is not all her fault. When she realizes that her parents' problems became her own, she may understandably feel angry with them at first. Instead of breaking away from them, however, she can form a new relationship in which she encourages them to nurture her in beneficial ways and discourages the negative aspects.

Darla's parents are both perfectionists, an occupational hazard for scientists. Darla is a perfectionist also. Otto Fenichel, a famous analyst, wrote in 1945 that people who are addictive "are intolerant of tension. They cannot endure pain, frustration, periods of waiting." None of us is very tolerant of tension, yet the tension is even harder to take if you are a perfectionist. First Darla is told that she must be perfect, next she is told that she must not have feelings when life does not turn out perfectly, and then she is shown what to do with the unbearably strong feelings that the whole family has: abuse substances. The normal pain, frustration, and waiting periods that accompany every person's day are unbearable and cannot be coped with if you have been told that nothing is acceptable except perfection, and that you must not express feelings when perfection is unobtainable.

Darla is truly a strong woman to be doing as well as she is, what with these impossible standards for living. In order to stop sabotaging herself, however, she must convince herself that no one is ever perfect. She could tell herself, "Perfection is not desirable anyway because we need to make mistakes to learn. I'm terrific the way I am and don't need to be 'perfect' to succeed."

Anyone who is addicted to anything feels deep down

that they need that thing to survive. That is surely the opposite of the truth. Not only could Darla survive without her "fixes," she could improve her performance in school, feel less stress around men, and feel free and healthy for the first time in her life. The initial step is to admit to herself that she is self-sabotaging through addictions, decide to give these up, and find people other than her parents to model herself after emotionally. In a supportive group setting such as Narcotics Anonymous, and with psychotherapy, she can learn new, more flexible, more compassionate, and easier codes to live by while she frees herself from her addictions.

Darla Fights Back

Two events forced Darla to take her cigarette addiction more seriously. A coughing bout worse than the first one really scared her, and the man she was dating said he couldn't stand the smell around her and in her apartment. He'd figured out that she was a smoker. Darla attended a group offered by the American Cancer Society, and she's trying to stop. She still uses marijuana, but much less, because she prefers to see her current boyfriend. A friend who is in therapy and Narcotics Anonymous has helped Darla to see what a perfectionist she is, and that there is a connection between her addictions and her family. Darla is beginning to believe that she might be able to survive without all her fixes, but for now smoking is all she can give up. She's proud of herself for making a start.

You can become addicted to anything, if that is your way of warding off your feelings. Arthur Berger writes, "A large number of Americans have become dependent on television and are, in effect, addicted to it but . . . [such] people do not define themselves as addicts." Most of us have minor food addictions. Certainly you know someone who is a "chocaholic." Many kinds of compulsive behaviors may be harmless in that they do not interfere with your happiness or emotional growth or cause serious health problems. However, when the addiction interferes with your relationships, your career, your health, your self-awareness and emotional growth, you are sabotaging yourself.

Weekends spent alone, a fight with your boyfriend or mother, pressure periods at work, being out with certain friends, a failed relationship—any time you feel rejected or unworthy or unloved: these situations can trigger your addictive behavior, which allows you to escape and soothe yourself. Work pressure because of success was the trigger for Helen.

HELEN

Helen, divorced and age thirty-six, looked like an actress with her frizzed dark brown hair, huge earrings, and vivacious style. What she really did, however, was work for a giant national supermarket chain as an associate vice president of marketing. The job had more glamour than it sounded. She flew around the country visiting the company's stores and making evaluations and recommendations, at first with her boss, later alone. She scouted locations for new stores and new food markets. Helen loved her job. She was thrilled by the traveling and was able to combine work with vacations skiing or sunning whenever possible. Helen hoped someday to have her boss's job.

Quite often Helen met store managers for lunch to discuss her report, and twice a year at least there were national conferences. Everyone drank a lot at these get-togethers, with much backslapping and joke telling. Many times Helen had too much to drink and suffered a hangover the next day. After a drinking lunch, she was half asleep throughout the afternoon. But Helen felt that she didn't drink any more than anyone else.

More of a problem, according to Helen, was her lifelong struggle to keep her weight down. Twenty-five pounds came off her five-foot-three-inch frame and went right back on again. She joked that she had more sizes in her closet than a department store had on its racks. Work didn't help this problem either. Gourmet products were tested each week, and Helen was expected to sample them. Helen felt right at home in this job because she grew up around lots of fattening foods. Her mother loved to cook for her four kids and her husband; rich sauces and desserts were paraded by Helen at every meal. To turn anything down was to insult her mother, and after all, the food was delicious. Helen won approval for clearing her plate and asking for more.

After Helen was at this job for two years, her boss became ill. She was temporarily asked to fill his position as a senior VP. Helen was told that the firm was giving her a big chance, and that they'd see what she could do. She was given a raise but was offered no help with the job. Helen had hoped to have a few more years' experience before anything like this happened to her, but she was ecstatic anyway and felt like an overnight success. She knew she was under pressure to perform well, and she missed having her boss there to reassure her, especially since all the company "sharks" were just waiting for her to falter. In her usual style, Helen plunged right into the job. Soon she noticed that she was plunging right into food as well.

Each night when she couldn't sleep, a midnight snack helped her to calm down and forget about work. Soon Helen's weight shot up higher than it had ever been. When one of the guys commented that the job seemed to be "weighing her down," Helen started dieting. Eight weeks later she was back to her prepromotion weight. But as her weight came down, her alcohol consumption increased. Too often Helen went out after work with the guys for a few drinks and then at home had a nightcap or two, to help her get to sleep. The drink calmed her as the midnight snack had before.

Helen had no social life. Her job consumed her. Work had kept her busy before her promotion; now she said it was impossible to find time to meet men. Helen had married early, when she was twenty. It lasted only three years because her husband had an affair. This scared her so much that she avoided getting involved again. Sometimes, however, when she'd had enough to drink, she'd bring a man home. At least it didn't take time from work. Helen felt she was in a catch-22 situation: she wanted to be as successful as she was becoming, but the price she thought she had to pay was drinking or eating too much, and giving up on love and family.

How Helen Can Win Over Self-Sabotage

An all-or-nothing woman, Helen does everything to extreme, whether she's drinking, eating, or working. She feels that she must choose between success and romance because her career is so stressful and has brought on the addictions. But she is not truly trapped, and in fact she *can* have it all. This will take much emotional work on her part, but she has everything she needs to have what she wants. These are the first, extremely important steps she can take.

1. She can acknowledge that she is hooked on alcohol, food, and work. She can decide she will stop drinking, one day at a time.
2. She can learn to understand how her smile-and-be-happy family helped her to become hooked on alcohol, and to work and eat compulsively.

3. She can begin to look at the feelings she really has and to realize that her addictions keep her from having a relationship.

4. She can accept that asking for help is healthy—that it is all right not to have all the answers in life.

The author Doris Lessing described the way Helen lives when she wrote, "She would have to live knowing she was subject to a state of mind she could not own." But Helen can own her own state of mind and be free to enjoy the treasures she is capable of reaping in love and work, as long as she can acknowledge that she abuses alcohol and food and is a workaholic. Her first priority should be to stop drinking, taking it one day at a time. Overeating and being a workaholic are problems that can be worked out over time. Helen must regularly attend Alcoholics Anonymous meetings and possibly also see a therapist to help her cope with her anxiety and other feelings.

Helen can remind herself of the following guidelines suggested by Valerie Levinson, a well-known psychotherapist in the field of alcoholism. She can use these words to soothe herself when she is upset about work *instead of reaching for a drink*:

1. It is enough just to talk and to start identifying problems—but nothing has to be done yet. In fact, it is better not to do anything.

2. Feelings pass.

3. The past is not a predictor of the future; we don't know the future.

4. Staying in this moment is safe; feelings are not facts, and are not dangerous.

Helen comes from a smile-and-be-happy family, sociable, well liked in the community, and determined to allow no "unhappy" feelings to interfere. Of course, families are only like that on television. In order to maintain this happy-go-lucky attitude, the family abused alcohol and food. As mentioned, Helen's mother prided herself on serving rich meals, which the family was expected to eat heartily and appreciate, or Mom would be annoyed. Helen's overeating problem stems from trying to please her mother. Helen's drinking patterns come from her father. Dad was well liked in their small community. He liked to sit and tell stories, but only over a drink. When Helen was a teenager, he encouraged her to sit and have a beer with him. These were the times Helen enjoyed the most.

To keep her parents' love, Helen feels she must live her life their way, abusing food and alcohol. Helen is an alcoholic, but she's denied that she has any problem, just as her family denied that Dad had a drinking problem and Mom was a compulsive eater.

All Helen needs to do at the moment is understand the origins of her addictive behavior so that she realizes she has no reason to blame herself. Later on when she visits them she will want to rehearse responses to the pressure she will get to eat and drink in the old family ways. Responses such as "I don't drink anymore, it was ruining my health" and "The doctor says I should cut out sweets" and "Why are you trying to get me to eat or drink when it's not good for me?" will help her to stay firm in the face of of family opposition to change.

Helen drinks to avoid feelings about having achieved success so quickly, as well as feelings about love, which she must keep hidden, feelings about dependency and intimacy, feelings like anger, competitiveness, and anxiety.

For example, when Helen was married she felt helpless and powerless to stop her husband from having an affair, even though she knew that something was wrong from the beginning. She let the affair go on because she felt she did not deserve to be treated well. Helen still feels powerless with men, but her compulsive use of food and alcohol, allows her to avoid dealing with this. She also avoids a relationship, putting off dating until she loses weight. She shields herself from social situations by working long hours and going to bars with guys from the office as her primary recreation. Thus she avoids any real relationships, so that she can avoid feeling inadequate with a man, feeling helpless with a man, feeling scared about abandonment.

Similarly, her brand-new success and the money that goes with it produce the following understandable feelings:

► Fear—that she is a fake, that others will be jealous and critical, that she will not be good enough, etc.

► Emptiness and loneliness—the feeling that she is no longer being taken care of, that she is on her own, abandoned by her boss.

► Anger—because she now must ask for help, because life is not easier but more complex, because she is being tested and not nurtured by the other executives.

All Helen has to do now is to be aware that she has many feelings and to observe how she avoids feelings and men. Friends, support groups, and a therapist could help her to look at her feelings and to learn to express them constructively, instead of through compulsive overeating and drinking.

Facing sudden success can feel like facing sudden death, even if it's what you've always wanted. There have been no transitional steps for Helen to use to get ready for this overnight change. One day she was the young girl in the office, her boss's pet, the next day she is a businesswoman in a powerful position. Despite the fact that she has lost

her "ingenue" status, she still needs advice and support—
a mentor, actually. Helen doesn't know how to ask for help,
or whom to ask, now that her boss has left. She fears that
if she does ask, the higher-ups will decide she is too weak,
too young and inexperienced for the job. Feeling isolated,
alone, and scared, she drinks and eats to soothe herself.
She overworks so that no one will find fault with her, as
well as to avoid social fears. As the pressure grows, she
may drink and eat more, just as many celebrities—Elizabeth Taylor and Sid Caesar, for example—have revealed
years later that they were at their most addictive during
the height of their success.

Helen needs to be told by a support group and friends
that it is all right not to know everything. She must find
sympathetic people at work to whom she can turn with
questions and anxieties. Helen must stop waiting for someone to offer help; she must take the initiative and look
around the company at the people she already knows.
Among these there will be least one or two whom she can
turn to for help. Her first step is to believe that there is
never anything bad about asking for help. All successful
people do it.

Success Without Compulsions for Helen

After a colleague told Helen to be careful because she
might become an "executive alcoholic," she woke up to the
fact that others were beginning to notice her problem. She
decided to start attending AA meetings. Generally, she has
been able to stop drinking, except for a slip at a business
convention and once at home. She's also considering trying
Overeaters Anonymous to help with her weight battles,
which are getting rougher since she doesn't drink. In a
burst of enthusiasm, she began a physical fitness routine,
but that petered out after a few weeks. The mentor problem
was solved more easily. The same executive who warned

her about drinking too much had had similar problems
when she was rapidly promoted. Helen asked her if she'd
mind answering her questions, and a working friendship
has developed between them. Helen is aware now that she
avoids men through her compulsive behavior. She met a
nice guy at an AA meeting, but she didn't feel ready to do
anything about it. A friend is trying to convince her to see
a therapist to help her with men.

Now we will now look at another form of compulsive
behavior, which may be more familiar to you—compulsive
lateness. Compulsive lateness is actually a kind of addiction,
though it's not usually thought of in that way. To most of
us, being late seems like a small enough sin. But like a sore
that is left untreated, when the little sin is ignored, it can
fester and grow into self-sabotage. A woman who starts out
being late to meet her friends ends up being late to meet
her boss or her clients. It's easy to ignore lateness instead
of seeing it as a form of self-sabotage, which is what makes
this kind of problem dangerous. You make excuses for being
late, feeling that others are wrong to complain, and that
they're making a big deal out of nothing. And all the while
lateness is causing serious disruptions in your life.

SHARON

At thirty-seven, Sharon was a special kind of kindergarten
teacher. Her kids adored her. She was the kind of teacher
that they would always remember. They loved her deep
red curly hair that formed a wild mass around her face, and
they loved her great laugh. And Sharon loved being in the
classroom, because she got to express her fantasies and the
silly side of her personality. She did this through storytelling. Sharon had developed a reputation as a storyteller;
she also told her stories professionally outside of the class-

room. Yet even though she was well loved at school, Sharon had her private hell to deal with each day.

Every morning she struggled to get to work on time, and yet she was always late. Nothing got her out of bed. Several alarm clocks and a wake-up service had all failed. Because she was always late to work, Sharon had to construct an elaborate system with other teachers at school who would agree to cover her class for her and punch the time clock. Of course, they asked for favors in return, which required more of Sharon's time than punching a clock. When all else failed, she made excuses to the principal. He had put critical notes about her lateness in her teaching record, along with the glowing teaching appraisals. But nothing had helped to change Sharon's lateness habits. The only events that she ever got to on time were her paid storytelling appearances.

Many of Sharon's friends lost touch with her because they wouldn't put up with her problem. Some remained out of loyalty and because Sharon was a good friend. But they all had stories to tell about her chronic lateness, like the time she actually missed the boat when she had arranged to take a cruise to the Caribbean. She flew to the first port, where she met the ship and her friends on board. The extra money for that flight put her in debt for a while. Sharon was routinely late for movies, dinner, to go shopping—a small sin, but annoying to others. Some friends told her off, calling her selfish and saying she didn't respect them or herself. Sharon felt misunderstood when she heard this.

Anne Lindbergh, the writer and wife of Charles Lindbergh, wrote, "Lost time was like a run in a stocking. It always got worse." So it was for Sharon. The blight of chronic lateness spread from one area of her life to another. It had already affected her marriage.

Two years before, Sharon separated from her husband,

Reggie. Although they had many problems, most often they fought about punctuality. Reggie hated to be late anywhere, and of course Sharon was never on time. As a result, wherever they went they would be late, and Reggie would be in a bad mood. Once they stopped having fun together, everything else crumbled too. Separated from Reggie, Sharon began to understand that her lateness was a more serious issue than she'd realized. Neither of them handled it right. She and Reggie had had dinner recently and their evening was more enjoyable than it had been in years. Sharon was on time, and Reggie joked that of course she'd be on time just when he had been prepared to wait. He even said how much he missed her, and that he wondered what it would be like if they tried again. As much as Sharon wanted to be with him, she worried that she could never be on time enough for Reggie.

Meanwhile, the principal spoke with her about a promotion to curriculum coordinator. This was a step up, but it would be possible only on condition that she improved her punctuality record. For four months Sharon was a changed woman, trying to impress her boss. But as soon as he decided to promote her, Sharon went back to her old routine, always being late, calling friends to cover. The principal was furious when he saw her, and she didn't know what to do. Sharon felt desperate about getting some control over her time.

How Sharon Can Win Over Self-Sabotage

The poet Phyllis McGinley said, "Time is the thief you cannot banish." Time became a thief for Sharon. She was on her way to being robbed of success, love, and the leisure to enjoy both. Rather than blame herself for being unable to control her time, which will only cause her more anxiety, Sharon should try these suggestions for defeating self-sabotage.

1. She should learn to understand how childhood power struggles with her father helped created the problem she is having now.

2. She should tell herself that all men, including her boss and her husband, are not her father.

3. She should recognize that she is addicted to habitual lateness.

4. She should realize that she is a stronger woman than she now thinks, that she doesn't need lateness to define herself.

5. She should allow herself to feel entitled to success and love.

The first and foremost reason Sharon is addicted to lateness has to do with her father, a powerful, exciting, and humorous man, but a dictator while Sharon was growing up. He was very strict about Sharon's time; he told her when she could go out and when to come home. Often his decisions were harsher than necessary, owing more to his anxiety about keeping his only daughter "safe" than to any meanness. But for Sharon, his iron hand was a red flag. The two of them argued vehemently every time an evening out was forbidden. Each argument ended the same way— Sharon would run crying into her bedroom, where eventually her father would come to find her and they would make up. These were some of their most tender moments together, while their arguing was terribly hard on both of them. Sharon's mother tried to intervene, but her attempts were halfhearted and she gave up too soon. On the evenings when Sharon did go out, she always came home late—to find her father and an argument waiting. As an adult, Sharon unconsciously now turns each relationship into a duplication of her relationship with her father: first she is late, and then she expects to have the kind of argument she had with him. She does this with anyone she feels close to or anyone she sees as an authority figure. Sharon should observe this happening in her life and relate it to her past.

Unconsciously, Sharon expects every man to be like her father—wanting to control her, expecting an argument, enjoying making up. Thus she battles about lateness with Reggie and her principal, who are the primary authorities in her life now. Deep down she thinks that they just want to control her. The angrier they get, the more connected Sharon feels to them, because this is the only way Sharon and her father could connect emotionally. Over and over, Sharon may have to tell herself that neither Reggie nor her principal is her father. She will have to remind herself that she is involved in a power struggle that, unconsciously, she thinks she can only win by being late. She only loses and hurts herself.

You can become addicted to the anxiety you feel when you are up against the clock, actually addicted to feeling bad—about yourself, and about others who are angry with you. If Sharon decides to conquer this problem, she will feel strange without the familiar anxiety, the passion of people who are upset about her lateness, and the usual arguments.

As with any addiction, she has to decide to deal with the feelings that will occur once she stops the habit, and to do this one day at a time. She should try to be on time at school one day a week, then two, and then gradually increase this. Sharon can learn to replace the negative excitement of chronic lateness with the excitement of being successful, admired, affluent, and having a satisfyingly warm and intimate relationship

Because her mother was a weak role model and her father was so controlling, Sharon thinks of herself as weak even though she is a strong and capable woman. Thus she is fearful of losing her identity when she is around others.

The power struggles that she gets into about her lateness
help her unconsciously to maintain a sense of who she is.
Being late, strangely, helps her to define herself. Deep
down, she feels that at least no one tells her what time to
arrive!

Reggie might have solved the problem if he dropped
out of the struggle and stopped complaining about Sharon's
lateness. Sharon would no longer have feared being con-
trolled and so she might begin to be on time. But Reggie
brought his own background into their marriage. He needs
a power struggle and a reason to fight as much as Sharon
does. A support group would help Sharon to believe that
she is stronger than she realizes. A group might also help
her to ask for what she wants in a relationship, so that she
won't need to be late as a way of asserting control.

Sharon does not feel that she deserves to have success,
love, less turmoil in her life, more peace of mind. She feels
that she should stay close to her parents' way of life—
frustrations, anxiety, arguments, power struggles. The
closer Sharon gets to having success or love, the further
she moves away from her father and mother, the more
feelings of emptiness and loneliness will emerge. These
feelings unconsciously force her to cause a diversion, a
commotion about lateness that then sabotages her career
advancement, and her love life. She needs to give herself
regular pep talks in which she says, "I am entitled to be
married and be admired as a successful storyteller and
teacher."

A Crisis and Then Some Improvement

The crisis Sharon needed to force her to make some
changes finally happened. The principal let her know that
he had given the coordinator's job to someone else, someone who was "more reliable." Sharon felt sad and angry
about being treated this way. She was so upset, however,

that she looked for help. She found a counselor, who is helping her see the power struggle that underlies her lateness problem and where it came from. As a result, she is late less often than she used to be. Sharon is thinking about changing professions, using her dramatic abilities more, as a storyteller and perhaps in acting. As it turned out, Reggie did meet someone else—but so did Sharon. And so far she has never been late to see this new man!

A SELF-EVALUATION TEST—ARE YOU SABOTAGING YOURSELF THROUGH COMPULSIVE BEHAVIOR AND ADDICTIONS?

Compulsive behavior and addictions can certainly be overcome, but first you must recognize and accept that this is your problem area. Answer the following questions yes or no to see if you are sabotaging yourself through the compulsions and addictions indicated. Remember, never blame yourself for your self-destructive patterns. Just seek help from any of the numerous therapeutic avenues available, especially the Anonymous groups. Observe the addictive behavior in yourself, look for the causes, and try breaking the habits one day at a time. You will find additional suggestions for conquering self-sabotage in the final chapter.

    1. Do you "have no time" to meet men because of constant long hours at work, working weekends? Do you feel relieved when you have to work on a weekend or evening because you don't have to worry about having a date?

    2. Do you say you have so much work to do that you can't find time to exercise, eat well, and get adequate sleep?

    3. Do you drink as your primary method of socializing with men? Do you have to drink to feel comfortable with a man? Do you have to drink in order to feel relaxed at any time?

4. Do you use prescription or other drugs to help you relax around people, or to relax when you are alone?

5. Are you in a relationship where your leisure activities regularly involve drinking or drug use?

6. Have other people mentioned that you drink or take drugs or smoke too much? Have you been talked to at work because of poor performance due to alcohol or drugs?

7. Are you jeopardizing a relationship or has a relationship already ended because of your alcohol or drug use?

8. Smoking, of course, is always bad for your health, but have you also ignored a doctor's warning that you should stop?

9. Do you eat to make yourself feel better emotionally? Have you had large weight gains and losses regularly? Do you often feel you have no control over what you eat?

10. Do you put on weight when you are with a man? When you are not with a man? Both?

11. Do you feel you need to use caffeine, other drugs, or alcohol in order to perform at work?

12. Are you regularly late to work or other appointments? Have you been warned at work? Have you ignored the warnings?

13. Have others complained about your lateness? Are you jeopardizing a relationship because of lateness?

CHAPTER 5

▼▼▼▼▼▼▼▼▼▼▼▼▼▼▼▼▼▼▼▼▼▼▼▼▼▼▼▼▼

MONEY
AND
SELF-SABOTAGE

▲▲▲▲▲▲▲▲▲▲▲▲▲▲▲▲▲▲▲▲▲▲▲▲▲▲▲▲▲▲▲

A fool and [her] words are soon parted; a [woman] of genius and
[her] money.
—William Shenstone

MONEY doesn't buy happiness, but most of us would agree
with Marie Lenéru, a French author who wrote in her
Journal, "If I were honest, I would admit that money is
one half of happiness; it makes it so much more attractive!"
Money not only makes happiness more attractive, it also
gives you power. Conversely then, chronic money problems can make you feel weak, insecure, and unhappy or
even miserable. As a result, you may not protect yourself
in your work relationships or with men because you feel
so scared, so powerless.

Money problems are included in this book because self-
sabotage is definitely one of the causes of women being
insecure financially. But it is not the only cause. Discrim-

ination against women—in the workplace, in the home, in
the ways legislation is framed by government—is just as
much a reason women don't have more money. The solutions to those problems will not be found in this book. But
the women I have spoken with over the years who sabotaged themselves financially, and the women we will look
at in this chapter, would have money problems even if
society was truly fair. Their difficulty lay in deeper emotional conflicts they had about being powerful and having
it all.

A hundred thirty years ago Louisa May Alcott wrote
that "men have to work and women to marry for money."
But today you most likely work whether you're married or
not, and you're probably as concerned about your finances
as any man. Yet now that you have control over your own
financial situation, there is equal potential for you to make
good money or to sabotage yourself through money. For
years men have been sabotaging themselves and their relationships through financial self-destruction. Women unfortunately can now do the same.

Financial self-sabotage may take the form of compulsive
spending, the habit that offers a momentary thrill that costs
you later. Or you may keep yourself in a low-paying job
because of your anxieties and fears. Or you may sabotage
yourself unconsciously just when you are on the brink of
making more money than you've ever had before, on the
very edge of success. The newspapers are filled with stories
of men who go from "boom to bust." We will learn about
a woman who fell prey to this syndrome as well, but in a
quieter fashion. First, however, let's look at Marion's story.

MARION

Marion's money problems began when she was in her early
twenties and she married Louis. She and Louis were always

in debt. He liked to have a good time even if they couldn't afford it, so on weekends they spent money. A new car, then a boat, a bigger TV, fine restaurants, flying south for the weekend—it was all fun until the bills arrived. Marion was supposed to pay the bills, just as her mother had in Marion's family. Only now there was never enough money. When their marriage ended four years later, Marion still owed thousands of dollars on credit cards.

Even without Louis to egg her on to spend, Marion lived beyond her means. Friday afternoons were her danger time. With her paycheck near at hand, the urge to buy something grabbed her as she walked down the street. There were so many beautiful things: cocktail dresses—which she'd never wear—gold jewelry, the latest makeup and perfume, and pairs and pairs of shoes, her favorite. Marion couldn't resist a persuasive salesperson, and she had good taste—which means expensive taste.

When Marion felt overwrought and penniless, she went to her mother for help. Each time they argued vehemently and her mother told her how irresponsible she was. Marion cried. Then her mother came through with a check to ease the pressure temporarily. Marion swore she'd never ask again, but she always did.

Despite this stress, Marion, who had been working for the phone company, changed jobs in an upward move: she began selling large phone systems for a private concern. And she made more money. For a brief period, she caught up on her debts. But as soon as this occurred, Marion spent again, borrowed again. She argued tearfully with her mother about her spending. Eventually she was denied credit everywhere. Her mother, however, then felt sorry for Marion and let her use her credit cards—after a fight of course. Much of Marion's time was occupied with her debts, so much so that one day she missed an opportunity to get a better sales territory because she was at a bank trying to get a loan. She was too preoccupied with her debts to think about this possibility anyway.

Didn't Marion know by this time that asking people for money caused problems? Apparently not, because she asked her friends for loans too. Marion had warm relationships with her friends, although she was often more tuned in to them than they were to her. Yet those relationships became tense when it was obvious she could at best pay back only small portions of the money she'd borrowed. Her friends even lectured her, the way her mother did. Frank, the man she had been dating for a year, made comments that were supposed to be jokes about not letting her get her hands on his credit cards. Marion didn't think he was funny. She was embarrassed that she couldn't get control of her finances and thought this might come between them.

There were many sides to Marion. Her spending sprees were there, certainly. But she also had a literary side; there was a hidden writer in her. She thought about changing professions and going back to school to finish her degree in literature or writing. But her ever-rising debts meant she couldn't afford school, even though on paper she made enough. Marion was tired of feeling poor, tired of arguing with her mother abouts loans, tired of seeing a future filled with more of the same.

How Marion Can Win Over Self-Sabotage

Shakespeare wrote, "He that wants money, means, and content is without three good friends." Marion is missing two of the three friends at the moment. She has the means: intelligence, ability, and the energy to do what she wants to do. But she never has enough money, and she is not content. However, if she is motivated to stop sabotaging herself financially, she can win. Here's what Marion should do.

1. She should admit that she has compulsive debt problems and attend Debtors Anonymous meetings.

2. She should become aware of how she is carrying out her mother's unconscious program for her and make a decision to stop this.

3. She should recognize that her money problems are a diversion from the real issues she faces.

Spending has become a compulsion—an addiction, in other words—for Marion. She seems to have no control over money; she spends in order to rid herself of unconscious feelings, to calm herself. It is affecting her relationships, her career choices, and the quality of her life, just as an addiction to alcohol or drugs would. Everyone knows Marion is a compulsive debtor, but no one is telling her. And just as with other compulsive disorders, the most important step for her to take is to admit that she has this problem. The next step is for Marion to attend Debtors Anonymous meetings. This group is patterned after Alcohlics Anonymous. There she will get the support she needs to stop her compulsive buying and the guidance she needs to manage her budget.

Marion's mother had yearnings for things way beyond the family's means. She would tell Marion how disappointed she was in her father, who made enough for them to get by, but no more. Since her mother didn't want to indulge her own expensive taste and wind up in arguments with her husband, she unconsciously encouraged Marion to buy only the most expensive things, without giving her any way to get the kind of money she'd need to pay for them. Then she belittled her for her spending habit.

Finally her mother encouraged Marion to be a compulsive debtor by paying Marion's bills, reinforcing Marion's dependence on her. Marion needs to recognize that her relationship with her mother is part of her problem and begin to observe how her mother unconsciously encourages her to spend. She can resolve not to discuss finances with her mother in the future.

Spending and the financial problems it creates provide a diversion for Marion. Her obsession with money keeps her from an awareness of what she really needs in order to do well. For example, Marion really needs people to take care of her emotionally, to listen to her problems and be understanding. Instead, she asks people for money, since she doesn't know how to ask for what she really needs. She feels taken care of when they talk to her about her spending problem or actually give her a loan, but she has had to sabotage herself in order to get this support. This is a diversion. She needs to learn to ask people for attention and caring without having to go into debt.

Marion feels she is too overwhelmed to take on a larger sales territory, too poor to be able to go back to school and become what she wants to be, an English professor and writer, and she blames her financial problems. But this is a smoke screen. What actually holds her back are her deeper feelings of inadequacy and the terrible feeling that she is just as much a failure as her parents were, as if being a failure in life was catching or inherited. She also thinks she is hopelessly irresponsible, because people tell her this when she asks for money.

Marion needs to tell herself that, apart from her debt problems, she is really a very bright and capable woman. She is capable of doing well in school or writing if she wants to, of handling a better sales territory if she wants that. She needs to be told by friends or group members that she is her own person, that she can be successful even if her parents weren't. After Marion is no longer being diverted by her debt problem, she can open the door to some of these buried feelings.

Marion's Debting Dies Down

The closer Frank and Marion got, the more he saw the seriousness of her spending habit. Thus he was the one to finally call her problem what it was—an addiction. He insisted that Marion go to Debtors Anonymous. Although she was angry at him at first, she is now grateful that he cared enough about her to say something. They have taken an apartment together. At DA, Marion has met other people with the same problem and has admitted that money controls her. She has worked out a budget, consolidated her debts, and begun to pay them off. Yet Fridays are still torture for her, and she has slipped off her budget a few times. She and Frank get into angry fights when this happens.

Marion has made some headway with her mother because she told her that she didn't want to talk about her finances or what she bought. But her mother questioned whether Marion really needed DA, and soon after Marion was back asking for money—and a fight. Still this does not happen half as much as it used to. Gradually Marion can see, for brief moments, that "debting" has prevented her from looking at the real issues facing her. And for brief moments she has begun to feel that, without debt, she may someday become the happy, confident woman that she has always wanted to be.

Having it all and then losing it was Janice's sad story.

JANICE

No matter what problems beset her, Janice was outgoing, bubbly, vivacious. Since childhood she tended toward being overweight, but that didn't stop her from wearing whatever was "hot," because clothing was her business and her passion. Janice's friends loved her and were up front about copying her style of dressing.

After college, Janice went to work for a large department store chain as a buyer. This was the perfect job for her. She learned fast and within two years was considered to be one of the best. For another year she saved every penny she could get. With a loan, she opened her own clothing boutique, her longtime dream come true. Because of Janice's unique taste and her way of putting people at ease, shopping with her was fun and flattering, and the store was immediately busy all the time. A magazine wrote an article about this young female entrepreneur. She was on her way up.

Janice met Clarence, a charming writer from this magazine, who was just as ambitious as she. They began to see each other. Clarence kept after Janice to help him start a new fashion magazine. She agreed. However, she at once put all of her profits into this project; when the magazine failed, so did their relationship. Janice now had no extra funds. When sales were slow for a few months, she was forced to close her boutique.

"You can be as romantic as you please about love . . . but you musn't be romantic about money," said George Bernard Shaw. Janice had to learn this lesson the hard way. It's easy for anyone to mix up money and romance, because both involve issues of dependency, but for Janice this was especially true.

Janice went back to work for a department store. Two years later she opened another boutique. Again, the store was an instant success. Customers increased monthly. Janice met Gerry, and married him soon after. Gerry was her opposite, quiet where she was outgoing, calm when she got excited. Gerry noticed that Janice was always short of money even though the store did well, but he didn't want to argue so he ignored it. It was not long, however, before

Janice was again in the red—with the landlord, suppliers, and others. She had to face the prospect of closing her store again, but this time her accountant, a family friend, demanded to know why. Janice broke down and cried, saying she didn't know what had happened. Her accountant looked though her records and saw that she set the prices on the merchandise too low and paid her employees too much. But there were still large sums of money unaccounted for. She confronted Janice about this.

Janice admitted that she gave people money readily. Any time employees, friends, or family members needed something, she gave. They were all supposed to pay her back someday, but so far nobody had. She just couldn't say no. As for her pricing policy, Janice couldn't stand not to have people buy when they came in, so she bargained with the customers, lowering her prices. And when employees complained about their salaries, she just gave them more money.

Her accountant said that she thought Janice had a self-destructive streak. She had seen this before. Janice thought this was psychobabble; after all, she had always been ambitious. If anything, Janice felt Gerry, content in his job teaching physics at a private school, was the one who didn't care about making a lot of money. Janice secretly was in a panic about her second business failure. She felt scared to do anything now, thinking that she must have been "faking it" all along. Yet she hated to give up the only dream she had ever had.

How Janice Can Win Over Self-Sabotage

Janice's accountant is right when she accuses Janice of being self-destructive, but she is wrong to blame her, because Janice is totally unaware that she needs to sabotage herself through money. No one loses money or stays poor on purpose. Unconscious forces are in control, until you become aware of this and decide to fight for what is yours. Janice has everything she needs to win, once she decides to face her problem and take charge of it without blaming herself. Here's what she can then do.

> **1.** She can learn to understand how her fears force her to give away money, and she can find new support systems to help her stop.
> **2.** She can recognize that when she gets intimate with a man she sabotages herself financially.
> **3.** She can attend Debtors Anonymous meetings or get other form of counseling.

Despite her bubbly personality, Janice has many fears buried deep in her unconscious that make her an easy prey for everyone who wants money. This is what caused her a financial mess when she was on the brink of so much. She gave money to Clarence for his magazine and to friends, family, and employees, as well as making deals with customers, because she is afraid that she might be disliked otherwise. She feels terrified by the idea that others might be angry with her.

An equally strong fear is that people will abandon her if she doesn't give them whatever they want. Since Janice thinks deep down that she is faking her ability and is an impostor, she is never confident that people want to be with her. She has to prove herself over and over again by giving away money.

Another fear has to do with her family. Her father criticized her mother for spending too much, even though her mother was frugal. Janice grew up being scared of him, and she still is. In a sense, anyone who asks for money becomes her father in her mind and might criticize her. So she gives in without a struggle. Janice needs to build a protective shield around herself, composed of a support system of people who are on her side and want her to have more in life. Her accountant is on her side; Janice should build from there.

When Janice gets intimate with a man, she sabotages herself financially. This is a problem for many women, because we tend to put aside our own needs in favor of caring for a man when we are in a relationship. A successful career woman may forsake her career, and thus her financial security, because of a relationship. But for Janice the problem is more extreme.

Having had very little closeness with her father, she yearns deeply for a "good daddy." As she grows closer to a man—first Clarence, now her husband Gerry—she hopes unconsciously that this man will be everything to her, will take care of her. She sabotages her success in the hope that he will take over. In this way, Janice emotionally becomes a child again when she feels intimate with a man. Poor financial judgment takes over, and she becomes a defenseless little girl being watched by her father, who was obsessed with and critical about how money was spent. She also knows deep down that her father needed to feel superior to women financially. Janice unconsciously thinks she must sabotage her financial security to allow a man [her father] to feel superior.

In reality, Gerry wants Janice to be successful—perhaps even too much, because this relieves him of any pressure to make more money himself. Janice must recognize that she wants to be taken care of by Gerry in some way. She should list specific things that Gerry can do for her practically and emotionally so that she can feel taken care of without having to sabotage the business that she really loves and doesn't want to lose.

Debtors Anonymous meetings will help Janice to stop making bad financial decisions when she is on the brink of success. They will give her the support she needs to be firm as a boss. Psychotherapy on an individual or group basis is another way for Janice to understand her compulsive behavior and to get the support she needs to change. Marriage counseling might be helpful as well.

The End of Janice's Boom-to-Bust Syndrome

Janice didn't have to give up her shop the second time. With her accountant's help and a bank loan, she held on until she was in the black again. Shaken by this near collapse, Janice went to see a therapist. She is beginning to understand that she is entitled to say no and to hold on to what she has made, although she continues to give money away every once in a while.

She also realized how angry she was at Gerry because she had to take care of everything, including the money. She has begun to ask him more and more to take care of household chores and to be more supportive and direct with her. His wishy-washiness, she realized, drove her crazy. As a result of Janice's new directness in their relationship, Gerry has been looking for a better job. Janice went to one DA meeting. She's didn't like it very much, but she is thinking of going back. She heard a lot of boom-to-bust stories like hers, and she knows she'll have to fight not to let her self-destructive tendencies sabotage her Midas touch as a shop owner.

A SELF-EVALUATION TEST—ARE YOU SABOTAGING YOURSELF FINANCIALLY?

Take the following quick quiz to see if money is your Achilles' heel. If you answer yes to any of these questions, your money problems are at least in part the result of self-sabotage. Use any of the suggestions offered in this chapter or in the final chapter to help you overcome self-sabotage. Do *not* blame yourself. Remember that your conflicts about money have been unconscious until now. If you are willing to become self-aware, you will surely be able to win your struggle to have love and success without financial mishaps.

1. Has your credit been discontinued in several places because of nonpayment of bills? Do you consider this to be "their problem"?

2. Do you repeatedly spend money that you don't have, as if you are compelled to buy something? Do you afterward feel anxious, despite the fact that you can't wait to spend again?

3. Have you repeatedly borrowed money from others, and have these loans caused friction in your relationships?

4. Does your mate complain repeatedly that you are causing financial problems, and are you ignoring what he says while secretly knowing he's right?

5. Do you never say no to requests for money from your mate or family, or co-workers, so that you are then without money yourself?

6. Despite your adequate or even good income, are you chronically unable to pay your bills?

7. Does some calamity occur that wipes out your finances any time you are close to financial security or even affluence?

8. Do your debts prevent you from being able to make career changes or other growth moves?

9. Do you build up a business or a career and then leave it or destroy it in some fashion? Has this happened more than once?

10. Are you badly paid compared to others in your field despite having ability? Do you do nothing to change your job?

11. Do you justify earning too little money with various excuses?

12. Are you secretly relieved to be poor because then you don't have the worry of having more?

CHAPTER 6

▼▼▼▼▼▼▼▼▼▼▼▼▼▼▼▼▼▼▼▼▼▼▼▼▼▼▼▼

EMOTIONS
AND
SELF-SABOTAGE

▲▲▲▲▲▲▲▲▲▲▲▲▲▲▲▲▲▲▲▲▲▲▲▲▲▲▲▲▲▲▲▲▲

WHEN ANXIETY, DEPRESSION, ANGER,
OR PASSIVITY DO YOU IN

▼▼▼

Concern should drive us into action and not into a depression.
—Karen Horney, psychoanalyst

ANXIETY, depression, and anger, in and of themselves, are
not harmful and do not cause self-sabotage. These emotions
are part of what makes us unique as humans. You're much
better off experiencing these feelings than pushing them
away; as Merle Shain wrote in her book *Some Men Are
More Perfect Than Others,* "it is the emotional that marks
our lives. One often learns more from ten days of agony
than from ten years of contentment." But for some women,
anger, anxiety, and depression are not momentary but are
a constant presence, sabotaging their efforts for success and
love or robbing them of the joy they should experience
once they have what they want. In this chapter we will look
at all three of these feelings, as well as what happens when

you act passively, as if you have no emotions. Let's begin by looking at a woman who eventually won against depression and anxiety.

LYNDA

Thirty-eight years old, Lynda was depressed, for an obvious reason: she had broken up with Alan three months before and life was not the same. Being depressed, however, was a common feeling for her. Lynda had days when she thought that she was talented or clever, but more often she thought that she couldn't do anything well. Even getting up in the morning was hard. Lynda always finally managed to get started, but the psychological struggle was exhausting. Lynda was an actress, a job that requires loads of enthusiasm and energy. When she worked, there was no sitting back with her feet up. Yet when Lynda felt depressed, just making meals for herself or shopping felt like a chore. At the opposite end, when she felt happy, nothing was hard for her. Lynda was self-aware; she knew when she was depressed, but she was not always sure of the cause.

Lynda had broken up with Alan because he refused to call her in advance about a date. If he did agree to a date in advance, he'd break the date at the last minute or he'd call late at night to announce that he was coming over. She knew she was right, and she was proud of herself for holding firm, even though he kept calling to see her. But in the end she thought that she had lost out because the relationship was over. He was happy and she was not. When Lynda had these thoughts, she felt more depressed. Soon she decided that there must have been something wrong with her if Alan wouldn't make the effort to treat her better, and that no one she liked would ever want her. Six months after the breakup, Lynda still thought this way and was still obsessed and depressed about Alan. She barely looked at other men.

Depression makes you feel blue, down in the dumps, hopeless or helpless. A sense of emotional paralysis can overtake you; you feel unable to do anything. You may think that no one cares about you or loves you, and that maybe no one ever will. When the feeling is strong, as it is now for Lynda, you may feel sure that nothing will get better, that you are a loser or at fault somehow. Your appetite can be affected, as can your sleep. Women admit to feeling depressed and anxious more than men do, and they seek help for these feelings more often than men. Women feel depressed and anxious because these feelings are the result of turning anger against yourself. And since showing anger is still not really considered "feminine," appropriate every-day anger builds up within many women and turns into depression. Many of the women I have spoken to over the years are shocked when they realize that their hurt, sad, or worried reactions also really masked a deeper sense of rage. Lynda, as we can see, is depressed instead of angry.

Less important events than the breakup with Alan would bring Lynda way down in the dumps too, such as when friends didn't call or visit as planned, or when she gained a few pounds. The events didn't seem to be worth all the pain she felt; she could see that. Lynda had done many commercials for TV, and had been been in a few movies and plays. She made enough money from her acting work that she only occasionally had to fall back on part-time tutoring to get by. Other actresses she knew envied her, but that didn't make Lynda feel better. She knew what kind of terrific parts she could get if she tried harder. Trying harder meant getting up earlier, going to more auditions, making contacts. When she finally got an acting assignment, Lynda felt great. If she worked more, of course, she'd feel better, but most of the time she just waited for something to happen. Lynda's the second oldest of five children, but only her older brother was successful. The others were talented but were worse off than she was.

Anxiety has different physical symptoms than depression. A fluttering stomach, pounding heart, sweaty palms, pacing, tingling in your extremities, shortness of breath, dry mouth—this is anxiety in its physical form. Psychologically, when you're anxious you feel that your secure way of being in the world is threatened, that your inner self is in some kind of danger. You may worry obsessively about a particular problem. Anxiety can run the gamut from just feeling jumpy, jittery, and edgy or having trouble concentrating to terrifying anxiety attacks. Lynda's anxiety was somewhere in the middle.

Anxiety took over for Lynda when her depression lifted. Once at an audition, the bigger the part, the more nervous she was. In fact, it was only because she was so talented that she had managed to get any roles at all, considering her high anxiety level. She could never sleep the night before an audition, and her heart pounded out of her chest.

Men made her anxious too. When she was with a man she liked, she felt very self-conscious and couldn't talk comfortably. Afterward she felt foolish, and anxiously waited for him to call. In fact, in a strange way, losing a man or an acting job made her feel relieved. At least the anxiety stopped. Despite this, Lynda had always had relationships, but inevitably they were with men she considered worthwhile but "flawed" enough that she didn't feel so insecure and inadequate. Alan had been better than most of them, and Lynda struggled with herself not to see him when he called at eleven o'clock at night. She felt that sooner or later she'd give in, just to stop her anxiety and depression. Maybe she'd better just give up trying to be treated well by a man.

How Lynda Can Win Over Self-Sabotage

Depression or anxiety come over Lynda so often that she feels blown off course, much like a bird struggling against gale winds. The normally hard problems in life knock her flat. Yet she can take wing again. Here are the steps she can follow.

> 1. She can become aware that her depressed and anxious feelings do not make her inferior to others, that most successful people have to overcome bouts with these feelings.
> 2. She can learn to take off her rose-colored glasses when looking at her family and she can choose to have a relationship with a man that is different from the relationship her parents had.
> 3. She can learn that she is not alone and begin to build a support system.
> 4. She can allow herself to believe that she is entitled to a "big break."
> 5. She can start an early-morning exercise program.

Lynda is ashamed of the depressed and anxious feelings she has and she is embarrassed that she stays in bed too long, is obsessed about her weight, and misses auditions. This is one of the reasons that she is not married or living with a man: she thinks he would not love her if he knew about her "problems." It is vitally important that Lynda change her thinking about her feelings. She should be proud of the fact that she has done as well as she has despite how awful she often feels. Being emotionally sensitive is an asset for Lynda as an actress and as a woman. Most successful people with strong emotions have similar experiences of sabotaging themselves in some form, wanting to stay in bed, missing appointments. These experiences do not make her inferior in any way. She has much to contribute to a relationship with a man and to acting, because she is rich with feelings. Once she has an outlet through which she can air what she feels and be understood, instead of toughing it out alone, this form of self-sabotage will stop.

Lynda examines her childhood through rose-colored glasses. As a result, she doesn't recognize that she was discouraged from being strong and was indirectly encouraged to be depressed in the face of conflict. Both parents were actors when they were young, but only her mother was still acting. Dad had become a psychologist, but was never successful. Lynda's parents fought a lot, and she always thought that they were unhappily married. Dad was a "nervous type," getting too upset to handle any problems the kids created. Lynda though that was because he loved them all too much.

Lynda's mother managed to make all of them except her brother feel foolish and wrong whenever they disagreed with her. To get on her good side again, the children would agree with their mother or change the subject to an interest of hers. Her mother always seemed mildly suspicious about Lynda's interest in acting and took an "I'll wait and see what you can do" attitude. Part of the reason Lynda feels depressed and defeated so easily is that when her mother did not give her encouragement, she felt she wasn't good enough. If Lynda looks at what actually went on at home, perhaps with the help of a therapist, she'll realize how insecure and threatened her mother really was.

Lynda never got angry at her parents, but when Lynda gets depressed and anxious she gets back at her mother in a very indirect way. She unconsciously tells her, "See what you've done to me?" and "I'm not going to be successful and give you something else to be proud about when you never told me I was terrific."

Lynda modeled herself after her mother when she decided to go into acting; she takes after her father by allowing herself to be only marginally successful. It makes her very anxious to think about being more successful than either parent, and this makes those auditions unbearable. And when Lynda becomes depressed or anxious in reaction to stress, she is also acting like her father.

Lynda doesn't realize that she is very concerned that if she were more successful than a man she was involved with, they would argue all the time, the way her parents did. But she *can* be successful and have a good marriage as well, just as many women do. Once she is aware that her parents have influenced her so greatly, she must resolve that her life will be different from theirs. She does not have to follow in their footsteps.

Lynda feels alone in the world because she has never had anyone there to help smooth out the rough spots. Because Lynda feels so alone, each time she is disappointed, rejected, or meets with conflict, she feels as if it is the final blow, rather than a temporary problem, something that might happen to anyone on the road to finding the right man or being successful. All the old hurts and disappointments come out to haunt her and make today's situation worse. She needs to develop her own inner soothing device, since her parents did not do this for her. She needs help and support to heal the wounds and learn to soothe herself, so she won't be overwhelmed by the hurdles she faces. She might also feel better if she realized that others have felt as she does, even though they may not admit it. Psychotherapy and a support group are two of the many possibilities that would help Lynda to stop feeling alone and debilitated by the unavoidable pitfalls she faces as a single woman struggling to build an acting career and to find a relationship.

Lynda will have to remind herself every day that she

is as entitled to her "big break" in acting as anyone. Being as talented as she is, she could be close to this point in her career. However, she unconsciously sabotages herself with anxiety just before an audition that might lead to the job that would make her rich and famous, because she doesn't feel she deserves success as much as others do. On a daily basis, Lynda should use self-esteem tapes (purchased at health stores or record shops) behavior modification, or biofeedback to learn to think positively about herself. An early-morning exercise class would help chase away the depression. Or she might try brisk walking outdoors when she feels down—always a good way to change your mood.

Lynda's Gloom Begins to Brighten

Lynda went through a rough year after she broke up with Alan, but she is coming out of it. She joined a support group that has helped her to stop feeling as if she is defective because of her depression and anxiety. Gradually she's beginning to feel angry about what happens in her life, instead of feeling depressed. Interestingly enough, as soon as she began to date again, Alan called, and now he sounds as if he'd be willing to treat her better. Lynda may have won that struggle. She is using relaxation tapes to help her before auditions, not that she tries out as much as she'd like to yet. But she is working out at a gym with a friend and looks terrific. She has also started acting classes again and is making some good new contacts, as well as having fun. Lynda actually got angry with her mother and told her that she ought to stop being so competitive and give Lynda more encouragement. Surprisingly, her mother is becoming more nurturing, at least for now.

Now let's look at a woman who seems to lead a fairy-tale life.

JUDITH

A stunning brunette and an elegant woman, at forty-two Judith was an achiever. Because she was a senior vice-president of a large mutual-fund company and dresses so stylishly, she has been featured in magazine articles on fashion in the workplace. She and her husband owned a beautiful terraced apartment, a lovely country home, and took vacations that other people only dream about.

Although Judith had been single for many years while she worked her way up the corporate ladder, when she was forty she met the man she'd been waiting for. Arthur was tall and striking with dark hair; he could have been her twin. An investment banker who worked as hard as Judith, he was even more successful. They collected modern art that fit beautifully in their city high-rise, entertained a lot, and were part of the benefit social season for their favorite charities and museums. To others, Judith was the lucky woman who had everything and could still be gracious and friendly, and who was always there to listen to a friend's problem. But Judith was miserable.

Judith had suffered from acute feelings of depression since childhood. As a teenager and young adult, therapy had helped, but the feelings returned. Years before, as a financial analyst (she got her M.B.A. at night while she worked), she'd had exciting successes. These gave her a high feeling, and she'd celebrate with colleagues. But once she got home she'd "crash," as she put it, and feel empty and more alone than ever. She'd sleep most of the weekend and not leave the house at all. Her only companion was her cat. During the week her work occupied her completely, but whenever she had any free time, the depression would start.

Then she married Arthur, expecting the bad feelings to disappear. But Judith noticed that these feelings had gotten worse since her marriage. She felt gypped when on a beautiful day at their country home she couldn't feel the joy she thought she should feel with Arthur, because the depression or anxiety interfered. She had waited so long for this; every day should have been great, she felt. Judith was very confused by a pattern she noticed—that a good day with Arthur could start her on a flood of tears.

At the many concerts, benefits, or dinners they went to, the smiling exterior that Judith presented covered up a jittery and restless feeling. When she was supposed to be relaxing, Judith's mind was elsewhere, occupied with her aging father and his failing health, or with work problems. Wherever her mind was, she felt anxious. Any complications that developed in her schedule—if she was tied up and late for a meeting, for instance—started her heart and head pounding. She felt as if she'd explode from the tension inside.

The novelist Shirley Ann Grau wrote, "It hurts to worry this much . . . It really hurts like a cut, or a broken bone." Anxiety and depression, as we can see with Judith, really do "hurt." She hurts while she feels this way, but then she hurts herself again because she can't enjoy what she has. This soon affected her marriage.

The marriage had its occasional tensions, but Judith felt incapable of discussing any disagreements with Arthur and withdrew each time. It just felt like too much trouble. Sex also seemed like too much trouble to Judith, because she often felt overwrought. Arthur was beginning to get angry and impatient, waiting for her to feel better. She was the woman with everything who felt as nervous and down as the woman with nothing. The more she got for herself, the worse she seemed to feel. Judith wanted to know what was going on.

How Judith Can Win Over Self-Sabotage

Barbra Streisand once said, "When people envy me, I think, oh, God, don't envy me. I have my own pain." Judith is also a woman that you might envy, yet she has her own pain, a very great deal of it. Her story may frighten you, because there seems to be no reason for her to be depressed and anxious. But there are definite causes for her feelings, and ways for her to gradually stop her self-sabotage. Here are my suggestions:

> 1. She can become aware that when her husband is nice, this brings up childhood feelings of loss about her mother that she has never expressed.
> 2. She can tell herself she is not crazy if she feels bad when life is going well. She can learn relaxation exercises, meditation, and other techniques to help change her mood.
> 3. She can learn to recognize that she is afraid of loss and to reassure herself that she will not lose Arthur if she talks about problems.
> 4. She can go for marital therapy.

Judith's mother was chronically ill with various heart problems during her childhood. After several operations, her mother died when Judith was eleven. Because Dad was often preoccupied with her mother's illness, Judith parented herself from an early age. Thus she never got the kind of caring attention she needed. When Arthur acts in an attentive and caring manner and Judith feels close to him, she unconsciously experiences the difference between what she has today and what she missed in her childhood, and in the years since. Thus she feels worse after an especially wonderful day.

Depression about being neglected in your past is often not experienced until the days of neglect are finally over and you are getting what you always needed. The depression Judith feels so strongly today stems from the neglect she experienced in her past, not from anything in her present life. Judith can now safely mourn the mother she never had. Once she understands this and is not scared of her sadness, the feelings should pass as she focuses on her full life.

Judith must accept that there is nothing wrong with her, even though, despite seeming to have everything, she feels the way she does. Unconsciously she has hoped that if she accomplished enough, it would make the emptiness from her childhood go away. But of course success cannot do that. Thus each time she's had a success she has felt disappointed and sad.

What Judith can do, however, is to be a good mother to herself now. She can use relaxation exercises, meditation, massage, and any other sources of emotional nourishment to make herself feel better. She should allow herself to enjoy the many activities she likes. She must be determined to enjoy the life she has worked so hard for, despite the sad feelings she has.

The more Judith has, the more anxious she feels, because the more she has to lose. Deep down this is her real fear—that all that is precious will be taken from her. She is especially anxious about loss because her mother was constantly on the verge of being taken away from her, and she finally was, through her death. This fear of losing all that is meaningful affects Judith's communication with Arthur. She is afraid to talk about the conflicts they have because she fears that the marriage will end, that it too will be "taken away."

Judith should tell herself that Arthur is not her mother, that he has given no indication that he would leave if there was conflict between them, and that she is not a little girl anymore. If she learn to express her feelings in the relationship, Judith will also lessen the anxiety and depression she carries within her all the time.

Judith carries many secrets, among them her desire to have a child. She knows Arthur prefers to remain childless, and so she does not want to rock the boat by discussing this or any other feelings she has. Part of Judith's depression is anger about this issue, anger she is keeping locked up. A therapist or marriage counselor could help both Judith and Arthur talk about the child issue, as well as how to express their feelings constructively in their marriage.

The Fear of Loss Slowly Fades

The family doctor convinced Judith that she needed to do something to relax, and she has started practicing yoga and meditating. Arthur, meanwhile, insisted that they go to a marriage counselor. As a result of seeing the counselor, they are each increasingly aware of how their family histories have affected their relationship. Judith feels more secure and less afraid that everything good she has will be taken away from her. She continues to feel sad during what should be happy moments, but since she is not afraid of her feelings and is not fighting them, the feelings do not last very long. She and Arthur are now openly talking about the baby issue—fighting might be a better way to describe it—but at least they're talking.

WHEN ANGER IS THE PROBLEM

Even though depression and anxiety can sabotage you, remember that being an emotionally sensitive woman is an asset, not a liability—as long as your feelings don't rule you. Of all the emotions, anger especially can be a lifesaving force when it is experienced and used constructively. But anger is often contaminated by other feelings, and we can get tangled up in these feelings when it comes out. The author Hannah Green hoped for a clean and direct expression of this anger when she wrote in her novel *I Never Promised You a Rose Garden*, "Besides, I like anger that is not fearful and guilty and can come out. . . ." It would be marvelous if anger never made you afraid or guilty, but usually it does.

Anger is also difficult to express because it's a powerful emotion, and like any source of power, it can be either a force for creation or a force for destruction. Although we will look at a woman who has allowed her anger to sabotage her, anger itself is not the culprit, it's *how* it is expressed that causes damage.

Women who defeat themselves through passive behavior submerge their anger too much. The woman described next had the opposite problem. Her anger, when it erupted, was out of control. Despite her tremendous energy, enthusiasm, and creative ability, her angry feelings, like a bomb, leveled what she had achieved, just as she reached critical turning points in her life.

ELAINE

Elaine, a "raven-haired beauty" with large dark eyes, was single at twenty-eight. She was also an art director at an advertising agency and very talented. But this job was her fifth one in four years.

At each agency where she'd worked, soon after an initial "honeymoon," nasty comments and looks would erupt from another woman employee. Elaine could not resist a fight, and eventually she and the other woman might end up name calling, even yelling. Each time the boss, usually a man, felt that Elaine should leave. And each time she felt outraged and hurt that she should be punished in this way. The instigator, always someone with more seniority, got away free. In some instances Elaine sent angry letters to the heads of the companies, but she got no replies. Her friends were sympathetic and told her that this was just the way people were in corporations, with their cattiness and backstabbing. After a few years, however, Elaine had gotten a reputation for being talented but difficult to work with.

Elaine certainly has a right to be angry in these situations, but she has weakened her professional life by letting her feelings pour out the way they do. Her anger hurts her with men also, as we will now see.

As a teenager, Elaine had attracted men who were pretty wild. They were all unreliable and mistreated her, disappearing after the first flush of excitement. Elaine would become enraged; she would call them and tell them off. In her twenties, she chose men a little more carefully. Now they were not all wild men on motorcycles, yet perhaps because she was used to being treated badly, even when one of these men did something she didn't like— let's say he was late—Elaine would explode. She started out nasty, quickly began yelling, and occasionally broke her own possessions. At times she would even hit the man. Fortunately none of them hit back. But the relationships all ended. Elaine told her friends that all men were impossible.

Recently, Elaine had been dating Phil. They got along well. Yet one evening she described a problem at work that made her anxious, and he was not sympathetic. Elaine became furious and struck him. Phil said he was not going to take that from any woman and walked out. For the first time, Elaine felt devastated and thought that her reaction might have been extreme.

The final blow happened not with a man but in the art field. Elaine painted whenever she could and had enough paintings for her own show. Through a friend, she met the owner of a well-known art gallery, who agreed to an exhibit.

Although the show was well attended, few critics or important collectors showed up. Elaine blamed Gladys, the owner, for not trying hard enough. She felt Gladys had put in more effort for other artists' shows than for hers. Boiling inside, she confronted Gladys, and an unpleasant argument took place. Elaine would not be calmed down by the fact that Gladys said she wanted to do another show in six months to build Elaine's reputation. Elaine just complained and accused her even more strongly.

By the end of the show, even though several paintings had sold, Gladys swore that she would never show any more of Elaine's work. Elaine's attitude at first was that she didn't need any snobbish thief in the gallery business anyway. But good friends suggested that she was cutting herself off from important business connections, and Elaine became worried. Everyone told her the same thing: her temper was sabotaging her.

How Elaine Can Win Over Self-Sabotage

Anger is a rich emotion, and should be expressed as a constructive response to dangerous situations, a response that helps you to protect yourself and define who you are. But in Elaine's life, because anger is wrongly expressed, it turns out to be disastrous, not constructive at all. She can, however, overcome this form of self-sabotage. Here are some suggestions for Elaine:

1. She can admit to herself that she feels hurt, scared, and insecure, and that these feelings do not make her weak.
2. She can resolve to remain silent when she is very angry and find alternative outlets to let off steam.
3. She can learn to understand that she acts as if she is in her family wherever she goes.
4. She can give herself permission to have a good life and to separate herself from her past.

Any time anger is expressed so explosively and in such outbursts, the outburst is always covering up feelings that are even deeper than the anger. Women know this from observing men, but it is true of women as well. Deep down, Elaine feels hurt, and scared, each time people do not act toward her the way she would like them to. For example, when the important critics don't attend her show, she is afraid of failure, and worse, she is embarrassed in front of the gallery owner, whom she so wanted to impress. She is not aware that these feelings are there, because to be aware of them would make her feel vulnerable, and she hates to feel vulnerable. She thinks of it as a weakness.

Elaine's angry outbursts are part of what therapists call her defense mechanisms, designed unconsciously to protect her from feelings that she doesn't want to have as she lives day to day. These defense mechanisms protect Elaine's status quo, no matter how bad that is, and keep Elaine the way she's always been. But Elaine really is strong enough to let herself be aware of her more vulnerable feelings. She will not be overwhelmed. Once she allows herself to feel her insecurity and fear, she will not have to get into confrontational fights to cover up. Instead she can build a support system and ask for the reassurance that she really yearns for.

Elaine needs to learn different communication skills to use when she is angry. This will take time. Until then, she should turn and walk away when she is very angry. She can ventilate her anger through physical exercise, even by pounding pillows, or through means such as talking to friends or joining a therapy group. She should consider how to express her feelings in a way that might get her what she wants, and return at a calmer time to discuss the problem, whether it's in her work or with men.

Elaine is always ready for a fight because she came from a warring family. Elaine grew up with her parents and older brother in a two-family house. Her aunt and her grandmother lived upstairs. The family spent a lot of time together, but much of that time was spent arguing. Someone was always fighting with someone else. Elaine's parents argued, her mother and grandmother argued, and Elaine and her mother had fights all the time. Elaine can't remember what they argued about, but occasionally they'd hit each other. Dad usually took Mom's side, but Elaine could count on her grandmother to sympathize with her. Quick tempers, noise, and turmoil were normal to Elaine.

Elaine thinks unconsciously that all people are looking for a fight as eagerly as her family did. When Elaine is quick to argue with women at work or to strike out at a boyfriend, deep down she feels they are like her mother and actually want her to fight with them, and that her boss is her father, taking Mom's side. She must tell herself that other people are not all like her family, that even if she is provoked she should not jump into a fight, and that she must learn to think first about what response will best get her what she wants.

Unconsciously, Elaine feels that she doesn't deserve good things because she argues and is "bad." This is what she was told as a child. As an adult, Elaine can see that she could have success, go to interesting places, participate in an elegant and artistic world that her family and friends from home would never understand and would think she doesn't deserve. This makes her feel very alone and separate from her family, and causes her to feel ambivalence about success. Fighting keeps her tied to her past. Elaine needs to find friends or a support group who will help her believe that she can have a good life and be separate from her past.

Self-Awareness Comes to Elaine

After the fight with the gallery owner, Elaine began to listen to her friends. Although she didn't think the problem was entirely her fault, Elaine decided it was in her best interest to make amends. She rehearsed what she would say and then went to see Gladys and apologized. Gladys was cold at first, but now they are talking about another show. Elaine has also started to jog as often as she can and to take long walks when she feels furious. A therapy group she joined has become a safe place for her to ventilate her anger. As a result Elaine has been able to avoid fights at work. She is considering changing jobs, however, because she continues to feel that the women where she works mistreat her.

Elaine also apologized to Phil, who was surprised to hear from her. They have been seeing each other again and trying to express their anger more constructively. Elaine finds this very difficult. She is not sure Phil is worth all her effort but is considering this a good "test" for her.

PASSIVITY MEANS SELF-SABOTAGE

Passivity has been an especially female trait for a very long time. Fluttering Southern belles, swooning New England matrons, silent peasant women sitting at the hearth are all captured in literature and art as symbols of femininity. And even though it is acknowledged today that being nonassertive is bad for women, many of us are, in some area of our love or work, still passive.

We are this way for very understandable reasons. It is a safe, approved way of life, taught to us by those around us: mothers, men in their various roles of mate or supervisor, teachers, and any number of others you encountered as a child or adult. Passivity is safe for many reasons. Though you may be unhappy, you will not be disliked or envied if you are passive. Others will not become angry with you, though you may feel depressed. As a passive woman, you don't have to worry that you are too pushy for men, although you may find that you are instead mistreated by them. A nonassertive woman doesn't make waves, doesn't make jealous enemies, and people approve. Yet when passivity becomes a way of life, a woman doesn't get what she wants in love and in her career, and then she faces a dilemma. This is what happened to Jodie.

JODIE

At thirty-five Jodie still had a soft, pleasant look with her fluffy light brown hair, a pink complexion, and pale blue eyes. Others found her soothing, but though people who met her remembered this quality, often they didn't remember her name. Therapists would say she seemed undefined.

Jodie thought of herself as wishy-washy and was envious of women who were powerful. By her age she had thought she would have had her life "together." But nothing was different. She was still single, still in a dead-end job, and so she felt worse. She tried to force herself to make decisions, but that just made her feel even more anxious, so of course no decisions were forthcoming. Her life repeated itself on the wrong track and she passively moved along through it.

For example, she realized that what had happened to her with the man she'd dated in the past year had happened to her before. She and Jeff dated regularly for six months; then she began to suspect that he was seeing another woman. Jodie never brought up the topic, and gradually they saw each other less and less. This reminded her of Paul, her college boyfriend. He had been perfect for her, because he always took over in everything. Jodie was never sure if she even said yes to their first date—or to having sex; it all just happened. They got along fine through college, but after graduation their relationship slowly fizzled out, in just the same way that she and Jeff had fizzled out. First Jodie got a feeling in the pit of her stomach that Paul was dating someone else. Jodie ignored her feeling, and the two of them drifted apart.

With Paul and with Jeff, Jodie blamed herself—she figured she wasn't good enough. She'd had news of Paul in the past year, that he was married with two kids, successful. The news depressed her. Several of her friends had recently married, and this not only depressed her but also left big gaps in her weekends. She felt she had been lucky to have friends who made social plans and included her. In the past year, however, Jodie realized she had stayed home a lot, or at best went to visit her family.

Jodie worked as an expediter for a large appliance firm; you might say she was an assistant to a division head. She had been there four years when she decided that the only way up was to become a salesperson with this firm. Finally she asked her boss about the possibility. He laughed and said she had to become a lot more aggressive. He recommended Dale Carnegie courses for public speaking, and maybe taking a business course, which she was already doing. Jodie felt devastated. She knew she should look for another job, or even a new career, but the energy drained out of her whenever she thought back to what her boss had said. Jodie felt the years wash over her as she sat unmoving, and her unhappiness grew.

How Jodie Can Win Over Self-Sabotage

The definition of the word *passive* also describes Jodie: "lacks initiative or forceful qualities; is inert, not active." Her passivity harms no one but herself, yet that is bad enough. Her life will be a series of missed opportunities, of "cruel omissions," as the British writer Elizabeth Taylor states. Her energy, untapped creativity, and warmth are wasted. Jodie can defeat this form of self-sabotage if she does not blame herself for her passivity, and if she is willing to work hard. Here's what she can do.

> 1. She can decide to face the fears and anxieties about success and power that keep her from taking positive action.
> 2. She can recognize that she carries around her father's criticisms, and she can learn to replace them with nurturant voices.
> 3. She can learn to take risks with men, to play to win instead of losing through silence.

Jodie does not know that unconsciously she carries very strong fears and anxieties about success that stop her in her tracks whenever she tries to get ahead. She does not know about these feelings because in Jodie's family she was taught that feelings were dangerous and crazy. Her older sister was either angry all the time or depressed and had even been hospitalized for this. No one else in the family expressed any feelings at all. So Jodie thinks she is crazy when she has normal feelings, such as anxiety about pushing herself forward to become a saleswoman. The only way she knows to get rid of the feeling is to do nothing, to stay away from success. She deals with the understandable fears she has about verbalizing her anger in a romantic relationship the same way: she backs quietly out of the relationship and leaves the fear of her anger behind as well. She must decide to face her feelings and accept them as healthy. A therapist could help her to explore her feelings, a career counseling group might help her move forward in work.

Jodie was afraid of her father's disapproval when she was growing up. He became judgmental and harsh when something went wrong, and she felt frozen with fear. It seemed her world would end. Jodie still carries her father's judgments within her. Whenever conflicts occur, she feels as terrible as he made her feel as a child. The child in her feels it is safer to be passive about her career or love life than to risk making a mistake, because she does not want to feel terrible. Each time Jodie starts to hear negative thoughts in her head, she must replace this with positive feedback. With positive thinking tapes and feedback from good friends, Jodie can build up an army of support and use it to counter the enemy lodged within her.

The author Ruth Prawer Jhabvala wrote, "Take me, make what you will of me, I have joy in my submission." Although Jodie does not feel joy in her submission, this is an accurate description of the way she acts with men. She feels she has no choice, that she will lose if she becomes assertive, but in fact she loses because she is passive and silent. Jodie must speak up about how she wants to be treated in a relationship. She should realize that both Paul, and Jeff became involved with other women because of their fear of relationships, and because she doesn't let her real dynamic personality show. She can tell Jeff that she wants a monogamous relationship, that that is what she thought they had, and he must make a choice between her and dating others. This is the only way that she will get the relationship she wants with a man.

Jodie needs to be aware that her boss is actually feeling competitive and is threatened by her desire to be a salesperson. He counts on her to be there for him. She should feel angry at his laughter, not take it as an indication that she is without talent. She might use his idea and take a Dale Carnegie course, but she should also bring the topic up again with him. If he doesn't help her to get ahead, she can either look for someone else in the company to help her or find a new job that will help her grow.

Finding Her Inner Strength

When her best friend got engaged, Jodie felt panicked and pushed out of her passivity. Jeff called again after two months of silence, and she told him she wasn't interested in going backward. Either they would have a monogamous relationship or they should break off completely. Since she has not heard from him, Jodie feels lighter and freer. She has been taking steps to meet other men and has had a few dates already with men who seem more promising than Jeff ever did. Jodie enrolled in a course in sales and public speaking that helped her to speak to her boss with more confidence. She told him that she felt he didn't take her seriously, and asked that he try her out on some sales calls as a test. She did well enough that he agreed to move her into a sales position.

Jodie joined a support group because she realized that she needed to free herself from her negative thinking, and because she is now anxious all the time about taking on this new job. The anxiety hurts, but she realizes that there is no other way. It's certainly an improvement over passively watching her life glide by.

A SELF-EVALUATION TEST—ARE YOU SABOTAGING YOURSELF EMOTIONALLY?

The following questions are designed to help you learn whether you are unknowingly sabotaging yourself through depression, anxiety, anger, or passivity. If you answer yes to any of these questions, this may be your area of self-sabotage. *Do not blame yourself.* Just being aware of self-sabotage puts you many steps closer to overcoming the problem. Utilize any of the suggestions in this chapter or in the last chapter, and you'll be on your way to winning what you want in love or success.

1. When a relationship ends, do you stay depressed about it for many months or years, so that you are inhibited from meeting new men?

2. Do you feel so angry at all men that this stops you from forming a relationship with any man?

3. Do you feel anxious whenever you are around available men? Do you worry if you've said or done the right thing so much that you can't enjoy yourself?

4. Do you feel depressed or anxious so often that you have no energy to socialize?

5. Do you think the fact that your anxiety, anger, or depression sometimes gets the better of you makes you less desirable to a man?

6. Do you blame yourself whenever you are in a conflict with your mate and other important men in your life?

7. Do you tiptoe around your mate and other men so that they will not get angry?

8. Do you react passively (helplessly) when there is physical or emotional abuse directed at you, instead of protecting yourself?

9. If you find you are angry all the time at your mate, do you do nothing to work out the problem? Have you gotten so angry at a man that you physically assault him?

10. Do you feel so depressed or anxious when your mate gets upset that you avoid talking about problems?

11. Do you feel depressed, anxious, angry, or lonely, seemingly for no good reason, when things are going well between you and your mate? Does this happen so often that you are not enjoying your life?

12. Have you felt angry and contemptuous toward others in most of the jobs you've held? Have you shown this anger in a manner that got you fired or held you back in your career?

13. Have you quit jobs more than once in an angry outburst

so that you can't get references and you don't have another job lined up?

14. Do you feel a constant high level of anxiety about your work, and has this been true with most of your jobs? Do you leave jobs rather than accept a promotion to a higher level of responsibility?

15. Does depression, anxiety, or anger regularly interfere with your concentration at work? Do you feel that you could be successful if you could only get rid of these feelings?

16. Do you act nonassertively (passively) around colleagues because you feel inferior?

17. Do you feel too down on yourself to make decisions about a career?

18. Do you behave passively at work because you feel bored and are unable to decide what other kind of work might interest you?

19. If you have become successful or well-off recently, have you felt either angry, depressed, anxious, or lonely for no apparent reason? Are these feelings interfering with feeling good about what you've achieved?

Part 2

FAMILY, FEELINGS, AND CO-SABOTEURS

Who and What to Watch Out For

CHAPTER 7

▼▼▼

FAMILY PITFALLS AND SIX SPECIAL PARENT TYPES

▲▲▲

"FOR better or worse": these are words that we associate with marriage, but they seem better suited to describe the family. You can leave your spouse, but your mother, father, and siblings are with you for life, for better or worse. You can choose your friends but you cannot choose the members of your family. As Samuel Butler told us, in families "people hang together artificially who would never naturally do so." Whether you are pleased with the parents you got or think yours are the worst you've ever known, your feelings about your family have been and will continue to be a powerful influence on your emotional ability to get what you want in love and in work.

Many women have insisted to me that this is not true

because "I have not spoken to my mother in two years" or "They live across the country and I only see them on holidays" or "My father died when I was ten; I can't even remember him very well." None of these factors weakens the impact of a mother and father on a child. How and why you sabotage yourself will depend in part on the kind of direct relationship you had with your parent, the quality of their marriage, and how they felt about themselves. It is the parents of your childhood that had the biggest impact on you, not the parents you know as an adult. Experience and age alter the ways in which you and they communicate. They may be better parents now than when you were a child, or worse, but your feelings came from your childhood relationship.

George Santayana wisely said, "Those who cannot remember the past are condemned to repeat it." Parts of your past you may want to throw out, other parts to hold dear. Either way, you should follow Santayana's advice and know your past to avoid repeating the mistakes that cause self-sabotage. This chapter is designed to help you develop an awareness of how families impact on children. In the latter part of the chapter I've identified six special parent types. We'll begin with Gloria, however. Gloria's story is an example of how parents unknowingly plant the seeds for self-sabotage in their children.

Gloria's father had been a telephone repairman until she was twelve years old. Then he died suddenly of a heart attack. Her father and mother had never gotten along very well, but still her mother fell to pieces. Gloria was busy trying to help her mother, but there was no one to understand how alone Gloria herself felt without her father. Her father was silent most of the time, yet she had found that comforting compared to her mother's constant criticisms. Her mother even called her stupid at times.

Money was never plentiful, but Gloria went to college. After her father died, she went to work for the telephone company, as her father had. She felt bored there and over-educated for the job with her three years of college, but strangely, she became panicky at the thought of leaving the phone company.

The social part of Gloria's life wasn't going anywhere either. She loved men—maybe too much. When Gloria met someone she was attracted to, she became obsessed with him, hovering around him like a bee around honey. Then he'd leave. This had been her pattern since she began dating.

Gloria does not think about what occurred in her childhood each day of her adult life. She does not realize that there is a connection between her relationship with her parents and the way she is stuck in love and work. But the connection is certainly there. She remains connected to her parents through what psychotherapists call *introjects*. Introjects are internal voices, thoughts, "tapes" that play in our minds as we walk, talk, eat, dress, play tennis, go on interviews, meet men, work, make love. These internal voices repeat to you in various forms the impressions, words, and ideas that were communicated to you by your family during the first years of your life.

These messages, delivered directly and indirectly, built the image you have of yourself, the way you think others see you, and the way in which you perceive other people. Your confidence or lack of it, whether you feel attractive or not, your willingness to be creative, make money, have a family, take risks, all depend to a great extent on these early messages, which you now hear as introjects. For example, Gloria's mother gave her many negative messages along with some positive ones. Her father's silence made him appear to agree. Here are some of the messages Gloria's parents conveyed to her:

- ▶ She is not smart.
- ▶ She is average-looking and vain to worry about her appearance.
- ▶ She is not going to be able to get ahead in life; if her father couldn't do it, how could she?
- ▶ Men are not interested in her.
- ▶ She is good at taking care of other people, and she should do that, because taking care of herself is selfish.

Indirectly, Gloria was told:

- ▶ Mother and Father will not love me if I am sexual with a man.
- ▶ Men are better to you than women. You should cater to men or they will abandon you. They might die if you don't pamper them.
- ▶ If your parents had an unhappy marriage you will be unable to have a happy one.
- ▶ Women don't have careers. They get married.

These are just a few of the many destructive "voices" that Gloria carries with her. Of course, Gloria received helpful messages from her parents too. She is well read because they liked to read, and she's interested in classical music and the opera because her parents were. Like them, she is a hard worker. However, to be prepared to protect herself against self-sabotage she'll need to recognize these negative tapes.

Here are several more examples of how introjects may work. Caryn's father told her directly how beautiful she was and Caryn believes this about herself and has always had men flock to her. But Caryn's father indirectly told her that he would be upset if she replaced him with another man, so Caryn has never had a serious relationship.

In a different situation, Karla's parents told her how smart she was and that she could do anything. Indirectly, however, they told her that if she couldn't immediately succeed at something she tried, it meant she wasn't cut out for it. She wanted to study music or law but since she didn't do well right away at either subject in school, she gave up both.

There are three basic ways that your thoughts about yourself (introjects or tapes) are formed:

1. Through direct interaction between you and your family, verbal and nonverbal.
2. Through identification with a parent or with both parents.
3. Through indirect communication of your parents' unconscious wishes for you to be what they need or want you to be.

Alice Miller, a noted analyst, asks, "How can you love something you do not know, something that has never been loved? So it is that many a gifted person lives without any notion of his or her true self." One of the reasons that women who are lovely and talented lose is that they do not have this important notion of their true selves. Your true self has never been loved or recognized. You were not born thinking that you are unattractive or stupid or that you're a bad businesswoman. Repeated messages, direct and indirect, unconscious and conscious, pushed your thoughts along one avenue or another.

In order for you to uncover your true self, you must learn to recognize those things that were told to you about yourself that actually have nothing to do with you. This would be the case when Gloria's mother told her she was stupid and that men wouldn't be interested in her. Gloria was really bright and attractive, but her mother was depressed about her own life. Unconsciously she made herself feel better by criticizing Gloria. She was also reliving her past—her own mother had criticized her as well.

Watch out for the negative tapes. Any negative thought about yourself that continues to reoccur over time should arouse your suspicion. It may be an introject, invented by someone else, with little to do with you. Thoughts such as "I'm wrong," "I'm bad," "No one will love me," "I'm unattractive," "I'm not smart enough," "Others will always win out over me," "I can't do anything right," "I'm boring," "I'm not sexual"—these are all introjects. We'll look at the three methods that form these thoughts.

DIRECT INTERACTION WITH PARENTS

"Kids say the darnedest things," TV personality Art Linkletter used to tell us. But parents say the darnedest things too. Out of a sincere interest in being the best parent he or she can, parents often make precisely the wrong comment to a child. Comments that are made lightly, in jest, or without much thought at all can weigh heavily on a child into the adult years. Within the walls of the family home, the words spoken by Mother or Father are the only truth you knew. Here are a list of frequently heard parental comments made to children and the resulting thought that leads to self-sabotage.

Parent Comment	*Resulting Thought*
"What's the matter with you? Can't you even do that without my showing you?"	I can't do anything right or without help.
"Are you *sure* you can [pass the course, ride a horse, etc]? It's not easy; it may be too hard."	I doubt myself. Other people are better, more secure.
"You're so [nasty, fresh, bad, sloppy, lazy]. You're lucky you have a family who puts up with you."	I'm worse than other people. No one will stay with me once they find out I'm so awful.
"Why don't you [get a better job, a better boyfriend, marry a doctor, move to a nicer place, change your hair, get married already]?"	I'll never please my parents. Nothing I do or have will ever be good enough.
Mother or Father or both rarely talk to you directly or don't talk about you.	I guess I'm boring, uninteresting, not attractive enough for anyone to care about me.

A look, gesture, or tone of voice can also be upsetting to a child and can make a lasting impression. "The coldness of my mother's voice on the telephone is the worst," said one woman. "I think I've done something wrong again."

As you search through your memory you may find that your siblings had more problems in their relationships with your parents than you did. This can still cause you to sabotage yourself in future relationships. Diane, for example, was never criticized directly by her father; her brother was the object of her father's put-downs, and there was constant fighting between them. Diane was afraid that if she said or did the wrong thing, her father would criticize her too. She heard his angry comments in her head long after she was on her own.

IDENTIFICATION

Imitation may be the sincerest form of flattery, but it can also cause problems. When a child imitates a parent and becomes a writer, painter, musician, doctor, or actress, this can be a good thing. Many families are famous for being gifted in some area. But sometimes the traits we get from our parents are not the ones we want or need. As a small child, you unconsciously identified with your mother, father, or both as you sought to define who you were. Today you may model yourself after the stronger parent in certain ways, the weaker in others. Sometimes the choice you unknowingly make has to do with maintaining a safe, secure role within the family. At other times, you unconsciously assume a trait that will help the family in some way. Jeanine unknowingly took on many of her parents' traits, some constructive, some destructive.

Both Jeanine's parents were professional musicians. The only question for her when she was a child was which instrument to choose, and she chose the violin, which her mother and brother played too, and the family got together around music, often accompanying each other. But their life was not altogether idyllic. Jeanine's parents discussed money all the time; her mother complained that her father was not doing as much as he could to improve their income. Her father was a member of an orchestra, but Jeanine's mother had always wanted him to pursue conducting. Although Father made promises, he inevitably developed an illness at the point when he might go for an interview or make important contacts. His illnesses were always temporary—colds, headaches, upset stomach—and went away as soon as the pressure was off.

As an adult, Jeanine also joined an orchestra. At the age of twenty-five she met and moved in with another musician, Bill. After a year, she realized that her boyfriend, although very talented, was not doing as much as he said he did to find work. She was furious and complained to him daily about this. His freelance work would increase for a while, and then he would slide backward again. Meanwhile, Jeanine was asked to play with bigger and better orchestras. She felt excited, but she began to have stomach problems, usually on the day of a concert or even the day of a rehearsal. She continued to be furious with Bill because he wasn't working as much as she thought he should. Jeanine's life was half pleasure and half pain.

Jeanine owes her talent in part to modeling herself after her equally talented parents. But in identifying with her mother and father, she also has taken on other, more destructive habits. When Jeanine becomes obsessed with how much Bill works, she is unconsciously imitating her mother. As a little girl she learned that this is the way a wife acts with her husband. And, as we all do, she met someone who is similar to her father. But Bill is actually more ambitious than Jeanine's father. If Jeanine—and Bill—is willing to become aware that they are playing out old roles, then they can change their relationship.

The other habit that Jeanine has adopted by identifying with her father, is *somatizing*, turning stress into illness. We all learn how to express our feelings, or not to, by identifying with our parents. Jeanine has learned to turn anxiety and anger into stomachaches rather than to express the feelings directly, just like her father did. Although Jeanine is moving ahead in her career anyway, the illnesses may eventually drain her energy. Becoming aware of how and why she sabotages herself will help to put an end to this family history of self-sabotage.

You can change the patterns caused by imitation. First, do not blame yourself. Become aware of what the patterns are. Alcoholism, drug abuse, violent behavior are obvious and much talked about syndromes that run in families. But there are many less dramatic personality traits, as with Jeanine, which you learned at home and which also cause self-sabotage later on in life. Observe your family and yourself, see what you imitate about them, and learn to reduce their impact on you.

BEING WHAT THEY NEED YOU TO BE

"I'll be what you want me to be," croon the love songs. This promise is supposed to be a sign of great love and devotion. Because of your great love for your parents, you may have become what they wanted you to be. The danger, of course, is that what they wanted you to be is not what you wanted to be.

Often a parent's expectations are obvious and stated out loud: "Visit me every Sunday"; "I want you to get married and give me grandchildren." Although these obvious expectations can be destructive if there is no room for you to be your true self, at least the message is clear.

The other and more dangerous kind of expectations placed upon children are the unconscious needs and desires of the parent. These are not stated outright. The analyst Alice Miller describes how this occurs in her book *The Drama of the Gifted Child*:

> There was a mother [any person, male or female, closest to the child during the first years of life] who was emotionally insecure, and who depended for her . . . equilibrium on the child behaving

> or acting in a particular way. . . . The child had an amazing
> ability to perceive and respond intuitively, that is unconsciously,
> to this need of the mother, or of both parents, for him to take
> on the role that had been unconsciously assigned to [the child].
> This role secured "love" for the child.

The "love" is really a sense of being needed and having a
place in the family, not love for who you really are. By
becoming what your parents unconsciously needed you to
be, you can develop the feeling that you have a "false self,"
as described by the therapist D. W. Winnicott. So many
of the women I have spoken to are describing this predicament when they say that their life is not what they had
thought it would be, not what they had hoped. A "false
self" seems to have been in charge. As a small child, you
may have begun to lose control of your real wishes in your
desire to take care of the unconscious needs of your parents.

Sophie, a twenty-three-year-old woman, was sabotaging
herself because she was obeying her mother's unconscious
directions. Although she had a college degree, Sophie was
working as a nurses' aide, a job similar to her mother's.
Sophie had over the years taken care of her mother, doing
much of the housework and listening to her mother's problems, because her mother would get very depressed if she
didn't pay attention to her. Her mother did say she wanted
Sophie to be "better" than she was, and she occasionally
told Sophie she was smart. But the unconscious messages
passed on to her from her mother were much stronger.
Sophie knew she must put her mother's feelings before her
own.

In order to make this confusing subject clearer, here
are two lists that state the kinds of expectations parents
may have of their child. One list describes the conscious
expectations, the ones stated directly. The other list describes the unconscious needs they placed on the child.

They consciously wanted you:
- ▸ to be attractive
- ▸ to be responsible; to take care of siblings
- ▸ to make money; to be financially independent
- ▸ to get married
- ▸ to have children of your own
- ▸ to be cheerful, pleasant, polite
- ▸ to be healthy
- ▸ to be smart and successful (go to college, be a "professional")
- ▸ to be a good listener
- ▸ to get along easily with people

They unconsciously needed you:
- ▸ to understand their problems and be similar to them, not separate
- ▸ not to have any negative feelings of your own, such as anger, jealousy, or anxiety
- ▸ to be smart, but not more successful than they
- ▸ to make less money than they did, or to make more money and take care of them financially
- ▸ to stay unmarried
- ▸ not to have children
- ▸ to be unattractive, or not as attractive as they
- ▸ to take on some of their emotional problems; alcoholism, depression, illness, anxiety
- ▸ not to enjoy sex more than they did

The expectations in the first list seem to be what any good parents would want for their child. The second list shows their unconscious needs and indicates that these same parents were insecure and frustrated people, completely unaware of their real feelings. They were unconsciously destructive because they did not choose to be self-aware or to improve their own lives. You may be sabotaging yourself because you are fulfilling either conscious or unconscious expectations or needs in order to maintain your parents' "equilibrium," as Alice Miller stated. But you are not "doomed" to be what they want you to be forever. Change is always possible, using any of the suggestions given in these chapters.

SOME PARENT TYPES

Trying to get an objective view of your family is much like trying to view the entire Grand Canyon: you just can't step back far enough. In this section descriptions of specific parent types are presented to help you get a better picture and determine how they are involved, if at all. No parent is destructive all the time, but parents who behave as described even part of the time over a period of many years can have a significant impact on you. The types I'll discuss here are:

- ▶ the double-message giver
- ▶ the mixed-up parent
- ▶ the abandoning parent
- ▶ the role-reversal parent
- ▶ the parent who fears failure
- ▶ the feeling-suppressor

THE DOUBLE-MESSAGE GIVER. This parent says one thing but means another. For instance, your mother insists that she doesn't need any help for Thanksgiving dinner, but then is silent and fuming as she works all day. When you ask her what you can do or if she's upset, she says, "Nothing," and, "Of course not." But you can feel the other unspoken, angry message: "You're a bad daughter to let this happen." If you have a parent who is a double-message giver, you feel unsure and anxious with people much of the time, instead of being the relaxed, fun-loving, assertive person you can be. You're not sure if men or colleagues really like you, and if they mean what they say.

THE MIXED-UP PARENT. This parent has weak "ego boundaries"; he's not sure where he stops and you start. A simple example, Father does not like mushrooms and you as his young daughter are served a dish with mushrooms in it for the first time. He tells you, "You won't like that," thinking that your taste buds and his are the same. You won't like mushrooms after this experience. It can be more serious, however, if Father yells at you for not studying hard enough. In truth, you're an adequate student, which is fine with you, and you study enough to have a B average. Father is yelling at himself through you. He failed to graduate from high school, and he cannot see that you are not him and your performance in high school is not as disastrous as his was. You feel upset because you feel that what you do is not good enough, and never will be. You don't know that every time he yells at you, he's talking about himself. You may become involved with a man like your father who criticizes you instead of himself and find that you believe his criticisms.

THE ABANDONING PARENT. This parent abandons the child either physically or emotionally or both. If your parent left you in another person's care for weeks or years, you may feel unwanted by others and find that you have difficulty with all separations after that. You may abandon others first, before they can leave you, sabotaging potential relationships.

Being abandoned emotionally by a parent is much more common. A teacher complains about you and Mother is not interested in hearing your side—you get punished. Your little brother bothers you constantly, but you are blamed. You feel unprotected in the world. As an a adult, perhaps you have a chip on your shoulder and find you get angry at people inappropriately. Or you take the blame for things that are not your fault, as you did at home, and as a result feel depressed, burdened, and unable to get what you want in work or love. You have trouble asking anyone for help.

THE ROLE-REVERSAL PARENT. This parent *needs* a parent and unknowingly reverses roles with the child. Your father, for instance, might ask you to make him feel secure in many ways, as if you are his mother instead of his daughter. Or Mother passively waits for you to make decisions instead of taking the lead. You take care of her, instead of vice versa. Many women have told me that they were expected to baby-sit for younger siblings at the age of eight or less. In fact they were the only available "mother" their siblings had. Being the only strong, responsible person in a family when you are still a very young child can help you develop into a responsible, capable adult, but women who have had this kind of experience often feel lonely, isolated, and unloved. Often such women are unable to ask for help and may become ill and overly fatigued at an early age, and they may have difficulty with intimacy. They may also seek out friends or a mate who has problems and wants to be taken care of, as their parents did, continuing the pattern of neglecting themselves.

THE PARENT WHO FEARS FAILURE. Because such parents fear failure, they make the child afraid of failure as well. Whether the subject is skiing, learning to drive, or math, Dad has no patience or interest in hearing that you are nervous or scared; you have to be good at everything right away, and like what Dad likes. If you learn slowly, get discouraged, or even dislike the subject, Dad feels terribly hurt and disappointed, and you feel worthless and ashamed. To avoid this, most children of parents who fear failure become overachievers who are themselves afraid of failure. They feel pressured all the time to perform and unable to relax, which puts them in a high-risk category for heart illness. They may have difficulty being intimate, become very angry easily, and expect others to work as hard as they do. If they choose not to achieve, they feel like failures.

THE FEELING-SUPPRESSOR. Because these parents are afraid or ashamed of their feelings, they suppress feelings in their children. Anger, jealousy, sadness, anxiety, and fear are the emotions most frequently avoided. For example, as an older sister, you felt jealous when the new baby got attention or gifts, but you were told by parents not to express this in any way or you would lose their love. If jealous feelings are expressed, they pass, but with this kind of parent the jealousy stays buried and can cause life-long conflicts between you and your siblings. Worse still, however, you will not allow yourself to feel jealous as an adult and may allow a boyfriend to cheat on you rather than risk losing his love. Anger is suppressed more than any other feeling in families. Your anger may have been silenced in many ways—by the threat of being hit or the threat of being unloved, often conveyed without words. As an adult, you may be fearful of the anger of others and retreat instead of standing up for yourself. Or your anger comes out in ways that are destructive to you, through silence or illness or explosive outbursts. Many parents show anger but do not allow their children to express this feeling. The child then may "rebel" in destructive ways or act like a "prisoner" in their relationships.

It may be upsetting to recognize your parent in these descriptions. It can help to know that most parents will have at least one or more of these characteristics, and that your parents are not the only ones causing your self-sabotage. Friends, your boss, the man in your life; possibly these people seem far more powerful to you now than your parents do. I will discuss how they help you to sabotage

yourself in another chapter. But your family was originally
the most powerful force of all, and may still be. Here are
some steps you can take to lessen the negative impact of
your family on your day-to-day life, whether you see them
all the time or only on holidays, or even if your parents are
deceased.

WHAT YOU CAN DO ABOUT PARENTAL SABOTAGE

Jane Fonda, playing the true-to-life role of the daughter in
the film *On Golden Pond* was willing to do backflips to get
her father's approval, even though she was certainly well
over thirty. We all continue to want parental love and approval even as we near the brink of love or success, but
there is much you can do to lessen the impact of a parent
who helps you to sabotage yourself. Here are some suggestions.

> ▸ Become aware of the many messages your parents gave
> directly and indirectly, consciously and unconsciously.
> Imagine that you have made a positive change in your work
> or love life. How would this life improvement change your
> relationship with them and their life together? If your par-
> ents are deceased, think of them as they were and build a
> realistic fantasy about what would happen now. (The mes-
> sages they gave you still affect you today.) Would this
> change cause a separation of some sort between you? Is this
> why you are sabotaging yourself?
> ▸ Discuss these observations with a sympathetic listener,
> a friend or therapist, or write them down.
> ▸ If your parents are alive, observe your interactions with
> them. Observe how you feel when you are with them, how
> you feel afterward. Do you feel happy, anxious, secure,
> loved, depressed, angry?

▸ Reflect back to them comments which you feel are destructive to you. For example, if your parents ask, "Don't you think it's too expensive for you to go to Europe?" You could reflect back, "Do I think it's too expensive? Why would I be going, then?" You might also add, "Is what you said supposed to make me feel good about my trip?"

▸ Allow yourself to experience internally all your emotions about the situation, whatever those feelings are. Decide whether or not to express them directly, whatever is best for you.

▸ Remind yourself that you are an adult now, not a helpless child. You have a right to have what you want in work and love, and if your relationship with your parents is changed as a result, you can take care of yourself

Katie, a woman who was about to be married, almost sabotaged herself because of her guilt about her father, but stopped in the nick of time.

Katie had wanted to be married and have a child since she was a little girl, but by the age of thirty-four this had not happened. Yet at thirty-five she fell in love with the man her parents had always said was for her—their friends' son. At the engagement party, her father seemed happy and healthy, but soon afterward he became ill. As the time for the wedding neared, it was obvious that her father would not live to attend the ceremony. Katie began arguing with her fiancé about details for the wedding. She felt impatient with him all the time and was critical of his every move. When he finally threatened to break off their engagement, she went for help.

Katie realized that she felt guilty and angry at her dying father. She felt that her wedding was "killing" him, and so she was unconsciously sabotaging her marriage in the hope of saving her father. She felt he didn't really love her anymore, that he must disapprove of the wedding if he had gotten as ill as he had. Katie felt despairing enough about losing him that she was willing to sabotage her marriage to save him. Once she realized why she was sabotaging herself, she stopped being critical of her fiancé. As well as feel her grief about his dying, Katie allowed herself to feel angry at her father for deserting her at this precious moment.

Katie's situation illustrates dramatically that when you feel you are losing your parents' love or attention, you may sabotage yourself. And the illness or even death of a parent, just as a child is on the brink of marrying or becoming successful, happens all too frequently. Even though Katie could not save her father, she was able to rescue her marriage by being aware and asking for help.

"Families are a given," says the writer Jane Howard. She continues, "Nothing is more futile than to wish they would go away. They won't." What can be made to "go away" are the negative thoughts and messages that were unknowingly transmitted to you. Whether you feel close to your parents or not, see them often or never, whether they are alive or deceased, this legacy to you exists. Once understood, you can hold on to what was helpful and discard the rest. This will place you miles ahead in ending self-sabotage.

CHAPTER 8

▼▼▼▼▼▼▼▼▼▼▼▼▼▼▼▼▼▼▼▼▼▼▼▼▼▼▼▼

WATCHING OUT
FOR THE
CO-SABOTEURS

▲▲▲▲▲▲▲▲▲▲▲▲▲▲▲▲▲▲▲▲▲▲▲▲▲▲▲▲▲▲▲▲

YOU can be sure that just when you stop sabotaging your-self, someone else will start. At times it seems that friends, lovers, aunts, uncles, and colleagues are just wait-ing for you to arrive at the brink of love or success so they can interfere—unconsciously, of course. Jane Austen thought that we expect or even need to have some sort of problem in our otherwise peaceful lives when she said, "A scheme of which every part promises delight can never be successful; and general disappointment is only warded off by the defence of some little peculiar vexation." Looked at this way, we could be grateful for these co-saboteurs, but of course we are not. They can be a pain in the neck.

Learning to detect the signs and signals that indicate someone else is sabotaging you is essential in order to have success or love. In this chapter we will look at these warning signals so you can be prepared for what hits you—and know what you can do about it.

Co-saboteurs are a tricky lot. They say they wish you well, but you feel worse after you're with them. Your boss fires you, your man has an affair—these are concrete, tangible, and terrible examples of being sabotaged. But more frequently you are subtly sabotaged by others through their emotional power over you and the comments they make or don't make. You care about a person, so he or she has the ability to get you to give up on yourself, to sabotage yourself, before you even know why things have suddenly turned out wrong.

What others do and say influences you for one very simple but powerful reason—you want people to love you, to admire you, to stay with you. You don't want your friend or mate or colleague to be angry at you, jealous of you, critical or aloof. You don't want these people to withdraw themselves or their warmth in any way. So you do what they want, think of yourself the way they think of you. You avoid conflict by agreeing. This might not be harmful if the issue were political. But the issue is you. Perhaps you agreed with your father when he told you that you didn't have the expertise to start your own business. Or you followed your friend's advice when she convinced you to "dump" your boyfriend because she didn't like him. Since there will always be someone who will disapprove when you get near success or love, you must be on the alert for these types of co-saboteurs.

The women I work with are primarily afraid that people close to them who react negatively to their success will never stop being cold, disapproving, or angry and will never speak to them again. Yet when these same women became stronger and refused to sabotage themselves because of a lover's or friends' and family's disapproval, it is rare that the relationship was lost.

The very feelings that cause conflicts can also inspire change. Jealousy and competitiveness, for example, can be motivating forces. If Janice is jealous because Susan was able to purchase a co-op due to her promotion, ideally Janice should be open with Susan about her jealous feelings and use her jealousy to inspire her to achieve the same for herself. Susan meanwhile should never sabotage herself and her achievements in order to keep Janice from being jealous. Instead, she should support Janice's efforts to get the same for herself. Unfortunately, not everyone responds as constructively and openly as this, and some of your relationships may deteriorate or even end as you overcome your own self-sabotage and improve your life. Do not blame yourself! Remember that deep feelings of inadequacy, fear, and hopelessness make co-saboteurs react the way they do.

Instead of ending relationships, it can be helpful to your growth to attempt to change the manner in which the co-saboteur relates to you, to change a destructive interaction into a positive or at least a benign one. Friends, lovers, aunts, uncles, and colleagues are often willing to stop their negative behavior, because they want a good relationship with you as much as you do want one with them. You may need to verbalize what has gone wrong many times before it goes right. Finally, if necessary, you may want to pull away from the relationship to protect yourself from the negative influences.

In each of the following sections we will practice recognizing when others are sabotaging you by looking at sample situations. I will then suggest new responses you can use with co-saboteurs that will protect you and also give them an opportunity to change. We will look at four kinds of co-saboteurs: lovers, whether boyfriends or spouses; friends; extended family; and colleagues.

LOVERS

The man in your life is as powerful an influence upon you as your parents, whether he's your husband, a man you've been dating for years, or a man you've been dating for a few weeks. His opinions, however, may not be in your best interest.

For example, men often unconsciously sabotage a woman's success because of feelings of insecurity and a need to be the center of attention. Mary Cassatt, a splendid impressionist painter, had a long relationship with the artist Degas, but he apparently had difficulties with her self-sufficiency. She writes, "I am independent! I can live alone and I love to work. Sometimes it made him [Degas] furious that he could not find a chink in my armor, and there would be months when we just could not see each other." This was a hundred years ago, and you do not want to have to go to such drastic extremes as not seeing a man for months in order to be your own woman. Yet a man's disapproval or negative opinion can cause you to sabotage yourself if you are not prepared.

There are numerous moments when sabotage can occur between you and your man. Even apparently meaningless remarks, jokes, or silences can have an affect on you. Women are often unaware that a comment has been destructive to them. Instead, they sabotage the progress they are making. The following brief situations are presented to help you to heighten your awareness of how your man may unknowingly help you to sabotage yourself. The first sentence describes an improvement you've made or some other positive event in your life; the second sentence describes common sabotaging reactions on his part.

▶ *You've decided to sing with a choir or take lessons on an instrument or learn to folk dance.* He says you're being childish

▶ *You're struggling to stay on a diet.* He asks you to pick up cookies at the store or sulks when you make "healthy" food, or gets angry when you don't want to go out for pizza or to fast-food restaurants.

▶ *You're thrilled because of a promotion or a raise in salary or a new account or other triumph.* He says nothing when you tell him, or he seems depressed or annoyed all night. He never mentions it again, talks only about himself.

▶ *You show him something you've written, or a craft you've become enamored with.* He finds something to criticize, has no words of support.

▶ *You've begun to handle the finances, and you feel good about this.* He tells you you're hopeless, "just like a woman," because you forget to write down a check one day.

▶ *You love to go out to dinner and a show but rarely get the chance. Finally you make plans.* He keeps you waiting for an hour before he arrives at the restaurant. Of course you miss dinner. He seems bored and preoccupied during the show.

▶ *You've made some new women friends and you enjoy going out to dinner and spending time with them.* He tells you they're out to use you and is in a bad mood when you get home from an evening out.

▶ *With much difficulty, you finally begin a new exciting career.* He becomes homebound, doesn't want to go anywhere. He might start to drink more, or get sick frequently. He loses interest in sex.

▶ *You go back to school two nights a week to finish that degree.* He breaks his wrist or has a car accident one night when you are at school. Or he starts a fire in the kitchen while cooking dinner for himself.

▶ *You and he have made plans to get married.* He suddenly

has an affair or has to spend weekends with his children, or stops having sex with you, or gets fired or otherwise sabotages his financial situation. He may get sick.

▶ *You're single and trying hard to meet a man and you finally do. You have a nice evening with him and he suggests that you get together next week again. He says he'll call.* He never calls again and doesn't return your messages.

As cruel and unfair as the men sound in these interactions, they are rarely sabotaging you on purpose. They are responding to fears and other feelings that are unfortunately out of reach of their awareness, buried deep in the unconscious. But when you are denied sex, are criticized just when you feel good, are kept waiting in front of a restaurant or by the telephone, the understandable response is to be furious. Many women do not feel angry when treated this way, however. They react with depression, self-blame, and too often they sabotage the creative endeavor, the diet, friendships, and even the new career. Even when a man is a relative stranger with whom you've only had one date, if he doesn't call, you may sabotage yourself by deciding that you said something wrong or feel hopeless about ever meeting anyone "decent."

Co-saboteurs do not force you to drink or eat fattening foods or bar the door to stop you from pursuing your career, but they provide plenty of ammunition for you to use against yourself. To combat the man in your life who is a co-saboteur, you'll need confidence and a strong belief that you are entitled to what you want in work and love. (Use any of the techniques and ideas suggested in Chapter 10, such as creating a support network.) We will now look at the reasons your man is destructive, and what you can say when he tries to sabotage you. You can survive interactions with him and still keep your goals intact. Even if you decide not to express yourself out loud, read the following suggested responses to convince yourself that you will not let yourself be sabotaged by anyone as you head toward having what you want.

Survival Responses

If, for example, he tells you you're childish because you've decided to take music lessons, he is probably treating you the way he was treated as a child. He is also threatened by the possibility that you will broaden your life and have a passionate interest in something that doesn't include him. You can respond with, "You're attacking me when you talk like that, and I don't like it. I think you feel threatened by what I'm doing, and I'd rather you told me about your feelings. Nothing will change between us because I'm taking music lessons."

Suppose you are thrilled by a promotion but he responds with silence and soon changes the subject to his day. Again, he may have come from a family who never praised one another, and so unfortunately he responds with silence out of habit, without thinking. His silence may also reflect anger or anxiety because you are moving up, or frustration with his own work situation. You can address his silence with, "I feel hurt [angry] because you're not telling me how terrific I am to have gotten this promotion. I'd like you to tell me that instead of acting on your anger or anxiety or whatever you're going through right now."

When you've had an enjoyable first date with a man, and he says he will call but doesn't, to call and talk to him would be a waste of your energy, because there is no history between you. Instead you can talk yourself out of destructive thoughts by thinking, "This man is obviously too terrified of a relationship to even be able to date. It's not my fault this happened, and I'm better off knowing he's so fearful before I got involved. I'll meet other men who are stronger."

Whether you choose to speak up or not, stay acutely alert to the fact that the man in your life can love you but still unknowingly help you to sabotage yourself as you struggle with work and love.

FRIENDS

A friend can be wonderful or terrible, a rescuer or a troublemaker. Truly nurturing friends are of course rare and are to be treasured. The kind of friends we are concerned with here are friends who, with their criticisms and judgments and jealousies, can help to push you over the edge into self-sabotage. George Eliot may have been thinking of friends like these when she wrote, "Animals are such agreeable friends—they ask no questions, they pass no criticisms." When it comes to friends, you need to build a semipermeable wall through which only constructive communications can pass. In this way you can maintain those friendships that have enjoyable components for you despite the same friend's negativity in certain areas.

For example, your tennis partner is a woman who is interesting and lively and adds to your social life in countless ways. However, any time you've discussed a work problem with her, she seems to be taking your boss's side against you. You always walk away from these conversations feeling terrible and hopeless about your career. Once you admit to yourself that even friends can sabotage you, it will be easy to see that she is destructive to you because she is competitive, or possibly because your boss is a man and she unconsciously always sides with men in conflicts. You will probably feel angry at this point. Instead of acting on your anger and canceling all future tennis dates, you can instead create that semipermeable wall around yourself: in practical terms, don't discuss work problems with her. The enjoyable part of the friendship will thus be salvaged and

you will have eliminated her as a co-saboteur. Sometimes
friends change and become destructive overall. You might
be better off ending this kind of relationship.

Here is a list of situations in which a woman may find
she is being sabotaged by a friend. This list will help to
heighten your awareness so you can be alert to the kinds
of dangers that may be present as you draw nearer to love
or success. Remember that the friend is usually not aware
that she is being destructive—she is not actually doing this
on purpose.

> ► *You have met a man and fallen in love.* Your friend
> criticizes him whenever you mention him, or she flirts with
> him, excluding you whenever you all get together.
> ► *You have plans to get married.* Your friend tells your fiancé
> unpleasant details about you and your previous relationships.
> He has been angry with you and there have been several
> fights because of the information she has given him.
> ► *You are finally happily dating a man, and you may move
> in together.* Your friend has become critical of you, tells
> you you're selfish, not as nice as you once were, and that
> he's having a bad influence on you.
> ► *You have just bought your own apartment.* Your friend
> has not called and seems cold when you speak to her. She
> says she's been busy.
> ► *You go to a better hairstylist and get a great, sexy hair-
> cut.* Your friend never mentions it when she sees you that
> week, though you usually compliment each other.
> ► *You've always had trouble with your weight. Finally a
> diet program is working for you. You look better than you
> ever have.* Your friend urges you to have some dessert with
> her when you go out to dinner. She says you look too thin
> now. Before she said you were too heavy.
> ► *You're trying to expand your social life, meet new men.*

Your friend says all the good men are taken and the rest are useless anyway and she refuses to join you in your attempts. You hear, however, through other friends that she's vacationing at a singles spot on the beach.

▸ *You have problems with the man in your life. You tell your friend about these problems.* She tells you to break up, get someone better, asks you why you are sticking with such a loser anyway. Or she says it's all your fault.

▸ *You have started a new career and it's going well.* Your friend never asks how it's going; she suddenly cancels a trip you're supposed to take together.

▸ *You finally get your degree.* She asks, "Are there really any jobs that you can get with that? I never needed a degree where I work."

These kinds of friends have very little, if any, self-awareness, which means that they don't know that what they are saying is destructive, and they don't know that they are impulsively responding to deeply buried feelings about themselves. They don't know that they are afraid of the improvement in your life, that they are jealous or competitive or feel inadequate, that they fear being left behind. You may question whether these people are truly friends. The writer Anaïs Nin said, "What I cannot love, I overlook. Is that real friendship?" You also may choose to overlook what you cannot love and may in fact hate. But there is another alternative—to respond in a constructive way to try and improve the friendship.

Here are examples of responses you can use when you are being sabotaged by a friend. The desired result is that the friend will reflect on her comments and actions, perhaps apologize, or at least stop making the destructive comments. The relationship hopefully continues and is healthier for you both.

Survival Responses

In the example in which you are planning to get married and your friend tells your fiancé details of your previous relationships, the friend is apparently upset or even angry about your marriage. She may fear that she will lose your friendship, and she may be jealous, especially if her own relationships are not going well. She may also want to feel closer or get to know your fiancé but does not know how to do this. You might say, "When you tell him those things about me, you are causing fights between us. I'm upset [angry] about this and would like you to stop. I think that you have trouble with your feelings about my marriage. I'd like to hear about them directly from you because I'd like to keep our friendship from being ruined." Another solution is to see your friend when your fiancé is not around and avoid the problem entirely.

In the example in which you lost weight and felt great but your friend urged you to eat dessert and said you were too thin, she is unaware of how jealous and competitive she feels because of your new chic look. Her mother may have urged her to eat self-destructively, and she's imitating her mother without being aware of it. She may also feel inferior about her appearance, and she may miss the days when you overindulged together, another family habit. You can respond with, "Why should I eat dessert after I worked so hard to lose weight?" in an incredulous tone, or, "I care about our friendship and it's best if we don't discuss food and whether I'm too thin or not. I know you didn't mean any harm."

When you are not especially close to a friend but she reacts badly to a positive change in your life, such as when you buy an apartment or you get a new and better-paying job, you may decide to discontinue the friendship. You are not trying to achieve martyrdom in your interactions with friends or with anyone else. Attempt to change interactions only with those people whose friendship is meaningful to you. When you give up on a friend you can console yourself about this loss by saying to yourself, "I need friends who will be happy for me when my life improves. It is a good sign that I am willing to let go of friends who are ungiving and to look for people who will give me back the nurturance I give them." Beware of friends who cannot tolerate your happiness or success.

FAMILY

Psychotherapists refer to family "systems," the network of relatives bound together by unconscious feelings, values, myths, experiences, and memories. The system can be as large as sixty or as small as six, but just as a pebble tossed into a lake causes ripples throughout the body of water, any change to any individual in the family causes ripples throughout the system. Parents are said to be the "architects" of the family, but other relatives certainly make up the building crew.

Your aunt takes you aside to let you know how upset your mother is about the man you're seeing. She is trying to maintain the status quo in the family system, a system that needs you to be single for its equilibrium. Blood is thicker than water, the saying goes, but it's also sticky: blood relationships create closeness, but they also create sticky situations. The writer Mavis Gallant noted that "no people are ever as divided as those of the same blood."

Women often sabotage themselves to prevent upsets in the family if a family member hints at disapproval. Families frequently divide over the issue of separateness: how much separateness can be permitted, how much individuality can be tolerated? If you want to be an actress in a family system that is used to doctors and accountants and managers, you may encounter relatives who will unconsciously try to sabotage your success to pull you back from being separate.

Family functions are fertile ground for sabotaging conversations with relatives. You should be especially alert for the signs of self-sabotage in yourself after any family function. My patients have reported feeling depressed and critical of all they've struggled to build in their lives after a family gathering. The men in their lives were suddenly repulsive, their jobs insignificant. Yet the day before, the world looked rosy. It is important to have a strong support system—friends, a support group—to restore your good feelings about yourself after family functions.

You cannot become an expert overnight at detecting sabotaging comments the moment they are spoken, especially at large family gatherings. It takes practice to separate your expectations from the reality of your family. It also takes a willingness to tolerate the angry and hurt feelings that arise when you face the destructiveness of the comments, the lack of support. Forewarned is forearmed, so here are brief descriptions of sample situations in which sabotage can unknowingly occur in families.

> ► *You are about to go on your first trip to Europe.* Your cousin calls to tell you that your mother is sick with the flu but doesn't want you to know because she wouldn't want you to cancel your trip.
> ► *You bring a man you're dating, who is a musician, to a family party.* Your uncle questions him relentlessly about music as a profession, his ability ever to make a living and to support a family.
> ► *You're supposed to be getting married in a few weeks.* Your father's sister suddenly dies of a heart attack. Your father is so distraught you don't see how you can get married.

▶ *You just got the promotion you've been waiting for for two years. You tell your cousin at a party.* Your cousin tells you how sick it makes your father to know that you are living alone in "that city."

▶ *You've just written an article for a professional publication, and you bring it to a family party because your aunt asked to see it.* The next time you see her you ask her what she thought of the article. She says she started to read it but never got the time to finish it. She asks, "Did you really write it, or do they edit it to sound like that?"

▶ *You are in a high-powered, well-paying, exciting job; perhaps you meet famous people, work with creative individuals, even travel.* At family gatherings, your grandparents and others only want to know when you are going to meet a man and settle down. "No man likes to compete with a woman," they tell you.

Although your relatives don't deliberately mean to harm you, still these comments or actions can create havoc for you emotionally, putting you into conflict about your goals and your abilities and making you prone to self-sabotage. Do not torment yourself after family encounters with thoughts like, "Is this man really good enough for me?" or "Will I ever meet a man at all?" or "I'm not really successful," or "Do I really have any talent?" Instead, think of responses you might have made, so you'll be ready for next time. Here are examples of responses you might make in some of these situations, and explanations of why these relatives act this way. The responses are designed to protect you without being nasty or critical of the relative.

Survival Responses

You told you cousin about your promotion, but all you heard from her was how sick it made your father to know that you lived alone in the big city. It is impossible to know whether your father is really upset or your cousin is imagining this or exaggerating a conversation she had with your father. She might feel envious that you are able to live alone in the city, or jealous because you have a more exciting life. She may also be remembering her own girlhood with a father who was overly strict and insisted that she live at home. No matter what her problems are, discussing this conversation with your father will most likely not be helpful to you. Assume that unless he speaks to you himself, he does not feel as she says he does. Assure yourself that you have the right to live wherever you want. Say to your cousin, "I'd really prefer that you not tell me things my father says about me. If he does talk to you about me, tell him to come to me directly to discuss this."

You wrote an article and gave your aunt a copy, only to have her ask whether you really wrote it yourself or had an editor do it. She is certainly jealous, but she's also unable to differentiate between you and herself. She would never be able to write an article, so she cannot imagine that you would be able to either. You can simply respond with a strongly incredulous question that reflects back to her what she has said: "Did I really write that article?" You might also ask her, "Why did you ask me for the article if you weren't going to read it?"

Be aware that there are numerous unconscious connections between all the members of your family which make each one dependent on the status quo for their own deeply hidden reasons. Use any of the ideas in this book to convince yourself that you have the right to have what you want, even if this upsets the status quo in the family. Using an extreme example, even if your aunt was to die just before your wedding and your father was terribly upset, you still have a right to be married. If you felt conflicted about whether or not to go ahead with the wedding, you could ask your father how he felt about having the wedding at this time. Even though he would likely urge you to continue as planned, you might still have to fight off feelings of guilt that could cause you to sabotage your wedding.

COLLEAGUES

As businesslike, fair, and just as any office or school setting is supposed to be, it rarely is. Petty jealousies and fragile egos too often run the office. What makes your work setting so difficult at times is a hidden psychological phenomenon that transforms the office or school or business into a family setting where each person is replaying old scenes, settling old scores from childhood. In such a setting each colleague can now play out his personal problem with you, becoming a co-saboteur and causing you to sabotage yourself.

Lillian Hellman wrote that "trouble in the world comes from people who do not know what they are, and pretend to be something they're not." When people do not know "what they are," they are unable to step back and see that they have been unfair to you because, for instance, you remind them of a sister who they never liked or a mother who made them feel constantly inadequate. As far as they are concerned, you are the cause. It is never helpful to "analyze" or explain this to a saboteur—he or she will only feel criticized and exposed. In the workplace more than anywhere else, you can benefit from a carefully planned strategy to help you through the politics and mixed-up feelings threatening to bog you down forever just as you are on the brink of getting what you want. Here are examples of situations in which women are often sabotaged by colleagues.

> ► *You have just made a huge sale for the company and feel this is the time to ask for a long overdue raise.* Your boss

pleads poverty, tells you all about his expenses, and never even praises you for a job well done.

▸ *You have been at the job a year and have just written a terrific report, which got a lot of attention at a meeting.* Your boss takes most of the credit for it, acts as if you are an annoyance that she'd like to dispose of, and rejects your latest promotion opportunity.

▸ *You have finally finished all your course work for your degree. All that's left is the thesis; the outline has been approved.* Suddenly your professor changes his mind about your idea, saying he wants something totally different. He does this several times without any apparent reason.

▸ *You've been working hard at the corporation and have been praised by higher-ups in front of others.* The clique that includes your immediate superior seems to be excluding you from their gossip sessions. When it's time for ratings to be given out, everyone else in that group is rated higher than you.

▸ *You're a teacher who's up for tenure this year. Recently you got married.* A man you've been friends with for years who's on the tenure committee starts to spread rumors that a project of yours was really done by someone else. He also tells people that your husband makes a lot of money, so you don't need tenure.

The danger in each of these situations is that you might attack yourself, blame yourself, feel that the colleague is right to mistreat you. By agreeing, you commit self-sabotage. Envy and competetiveness are obviously the primary reasons why these co-saboteurs act the way they do. They have lived their lives feeling jealous and mistreating others without any self-awareness. The only wrong you have done them is to have excelled. Shakespeare wonderfully described these people, warning us not to react similarly:

> **Jealous souls will not be answer'd so;**
> **They are not ever jealous for the cause,**
> **But jealous for they are jealous.**

Feelings of deep but denied insecurity and inadequacy also cause colleagues to sabotage you, as when a boss takes credit for your work. You might be afraid that you will be fired or given a poor grade if you discuss the problem with your boss or teacher. There is no one solution. Whether or not you choose to confront the individual, realizing that you are being sabotaged only because you are finally getting what you've worked for will help to bolster your confidence level.

It may sound surprising but with this group of co-saboteurs, it is unwise to express your own anger, hurt, or anxiety because these feelings will be misunderstood and possibly used against you. Go to a friend, a therapist, or a support group to ventilate your anger. And if, as in the example, your boss took credit for a report and did not give you a promotion, you can use your anger to motivate you to find a new job or a position within the company with a more generous and nurturing supervisor.

In the example in which the man who had been a friend spread rumors to prevent you from getting tenure, you might confront him directly by saying, "How come you are trying to sabotage me after we've been friends all these years? If you've got some negative feelings toward me, I'd rather hear them directly, not through the stories you're telling."

Any time you become successful, acquire possessions, feel self-confident, or find a loving relationship, there will be co-saboteurs just waiting to rock the boat that you have worked hard to keep afloat. Their sabotage of you is hardly personal; they would react this way toward anyone who had been able to do what you've done. Stay aware of co-saboteurs, and be determined not to sabotage yourself because of others. This will keep you on track toward your goals. When you feel compelled to get back at these troublemakers, remember these famous words: "Living well is the best revenge."

▼▼▼▼▼▼▼▼▼▼▼▼▼▼▼▼▼▼▼▼▼▼▼▼▼▼▼▼▼▼▼▼▼▼

CHAPTER 9

FEELINGS TO WATCH OUT FOR ON THE BRINK OF LOVE OR SUCCESS

▲▲▲▲▲▲▲▲▲▲▲▲▲▲▲▲▲▲▲▲▲▲▲▲▲▲▲▲▲▲▲▲▲▲▲▲▲

FEELINGS about love and success that have been buried are pushed to the surface when you finally begin to get what you want. A new job puts you in charge of other people and you are forced to realize how scared you are to be "the boss," even though you always wanted this. Or you actually meet a man who will make a commitment and suddenly you see how anxious you become. The feelings that surface at these moments are familiar, but you have probably not connected success and love with them. These feelings are anxiety, disappointment and disillusionment, emptiness, fear, loneliness, guilt, and anger.

Wait a minute, you may protest, these emotions don't

go with having it all. But in fact they do. We'll look at each feeling and see why you may be experiencing it even though everything's going right. Don't be discouraged! When these feelings occur as a result of getting what you want, they don't usually last long. They come and go quickly and shouldn't hurt what you've achieved.

ANXIETY

To feel anxiety is to be "troubled and uneasy in mind." Why feel like that if you are beginning to get what you want? The analyst Rollo May's definition makes it clear why you might feel anxiety on the brink of love or success: anxiety is the reaction you have when any pattern you've developed in life and on which you depend seems to be threatened. Thus when you meet success or love head on, the patterns of your life must of course be disrupted and even threatened by the entirely new situation, no matter ow much you have wished for the event.

The result of the changes that occur in your daily patterns has to produce anxiety in you. Even anticipating these changes or imagining them can make you feel anxious, because you know that your life will be different if you get what you want. A common example of this can be seen when a single woman becomes involved with a man or marries him. Suddenly she sees her friends less often, they resent her happiness, she speaks to her mother less frequently on the phone, has less time for her work, feels many new pressures. The changes are even more dramatic when a woman has a child. Feelings of anxiety as a result of these events are not only understandable but even appropriate, because the patterns of life on which you have depended are now totally disrupted. Buying a home is wonderful, but this too causes a disruption.

Thus anxiety occurs because of disruptions to your safe life.

There is another place that your anxiety can come from as you begin to achieve success. W. H. Auden described this situation beautifully: "Alive but alone, belonging—where? Unattached as tumbleweed." Being disconnected from your old sources of protection and care is extremely anxiety-provoking, and this is precisely what happens when you become successful, as Sarah discovered.

After six years working in a large teaching hospital as a physical therapist, Sarah wanted to earn more and have greater freedom in her hours. She hoped to have a family when she and her boyfriend felt ready, and having a business of her own made the most sense to her. She opened her own office and began to work there in the evenings with her own patients. A year later she was ready to go at this full-time, so she left her job and became self-employed. Sarah had been prepared for the anxiety about money—would she see enough patients each week to pay the rent?—and the anxiety about taking on so much personal responsibility. But she was unprepared for the onslaught of constant nervous tension she felt every day, and which seemed to have no cause. She wasn't sleeping well, and her jaws ached from grinding her teeth at night. Her patients liked her, and she was able to handle their problems, but it didn't help to ease her anxiety. She thought seriously about giving up her practice and going back to her old job.

Sarah feels "unattached as tumbleweed." She no longer sees her friends from the hospital every day, as she used to, no longer has the camaraderie of meetings and discussions with the other professionals. But this alone would not cause so much anxiety. What produces the unbearable tension is that she feels as if she has lost her family, both her real one and the family that the hospital represented to

her, whether she knew it or not. As a child she was expected
to be self-sufficient early on, which she managed, but with
much anxiety. When she occasionally collapsed, physically
or, later on, financially, her parents would provide some
sort of assistance. In addition, her mother had been ill a
lot when Sarah was young, and she was unavailable to take
care of Sarah for a year. Being alone in an office is stirring
up the old feeling that she is without anyone who really
cares about her, almost as if she is a child without parents
again.

Anxiety can stem from feeling cut off from family,
friends, and old colleagues when you become successful,
and it can be intensified if you've never really felt protected to begin with. Sarah should become aware of the
source of this anxiety and realize that it is an old feeling
that need not control her now in the present. She can
look for new sources of nurturance and emotional
contact—getting together with colleagues, friends, perhaps teaching or joining a group practice—to replace the
hospital setting.

Love brings its own special reason for anxiety: being
close to a man leaves you open to being hurt, rejected, or
abandoned. Many women—and men—unconsciously sabotage their possibilities for a relationship rather than experience this anxiety. This anxiety can be especially strong
if you have been abandoned or rejected in some way as a
child. If you feel especially anxious about being left when
you are with a man, seek therapeutic help so you can relax
and enjoy the relationship.

Thus anxiety when you have achieved success or love
can be caused by: the disruption of old safe patterns, by
being disconnected from childhood and other sources of
protection, and by the possibility of rejection or abandonment. Remember, it's only a feeling. It will pass. If it
doesn't, find a source of counseling.

DISAPPOINTMENT AND DISILLUSIONMENT

Disappointment is the feeling that arises when you fail to get what you had hoped for, expected, or desired. Isak Dinesen wrote of one of her characters in *Winters' Tales*: "But she was badly hurt and disappointed because the world was not a much greater place . . . and because nothing more colossal, more like the dramas of the stage, took place in it." From the time of childhood or early adult years, goals that you set for yourself seem magical: the money to have the things you want, a relationship in which you will be loved, a chosen career. But most often, as you attain or get close to those goals, the world does not appear to be "a much greater place," "colossal." What we have achieved is not magical now but real, with all that that implies. Disappointment is understandable.

Another kind of disappointment comes over women who suffer from the imposter syndrome, who feel like "frauds" or "phonies" their whole lives and expect that a degree or a child or some new status will eliminate that feeling, only to find that it doesn't. This fraudulent feeling comes and goes for most of us, but if it plagues you, you should go for help.

Disillusionment is a close cousin of disappointment. To be disillusioned is to be "set free from pleasant but mistaken beliefs." When you have to let go of a pleasant belief that has proved false, you may feel betrayed. An entire way of thinking that has allowed you to feel safe and protected for years is gone. You may feel that you have been fed a line. Patsy is a woman who almost quit an important job and gave up on a relationship because she felt so disappointed and disillusioned.

As soon as she got her law degree Patsy managed to get a high-paying job in a prestigious law firm. This was her dream come true. She finally had enough money to pay off some loans and live better than she had in years. Her boyfriend was a lawyer too, and they seemed perfectly compatible. Patsy worked for George, one of the firm's partners. She openly idolized him. He patiently taught her the ropes and praised the assignments she turned in. Patsy worked long hours, but she felt that George was such a great boss it was worth it. The shattering of her balloon took place late one afternoon when George called her in to go over her first-year review. He said her work had been "average," and although he could have recommended that she be made an associate in the firm, he thought she needed another year of training with him before that would happen. Patsy was devastated. She protested mildly and cried.

At home that night she also cried to her boyfriend, Ken, who was totally unsympathetic and told her she had to be tough in the real world and that maybe her boss was right. Patsy felt so despairing that she couldn't go in to work the next day. She thought she might quit the field of law altogether if all she could be was average. She didn't realize how angry, disappointed, and disillusioned she was with both her boyfriend and her boss.

Fortunately a woman friend who was also a lawyer talked to her. She was encouraging about Patsy's abilities and told her she had been through a similar situation. She told Patsy it was very clear that her boss wanted to hold her back only because he liked having her around. Patsy looked up to him and fed his ego. Once she was promoted, she might not work for him anymore. She convinced Patsy not to quit immediately, because it would be self-destructive, and convinced her to look for someone else in the firm to work for. Patsy had to realize that George was not the perfect protector. Patsy knew that what her friend said was true and began to plan how to take care of herself at the firm. She also told Ken that she was angry and wanted him to be supportive of her abilities in the future.

In Patsy's situation, her disillusionment at work was intensified by her relationship with her parents. Her mother was an alcoholic; she promised Patsy many things and usually did not follow through. Patsy grew up yearning for a good parent who would keep her promises. Patsy has years of deeply buried disappointments and her reaction to her boss is intensified by these deep feelings about the way her mother treated her.

Even when you do get what you want you may feel disappointed and disillusioned. Don't let the feelings overwhelm you or cause you to sabotage yourself. Understand them, give yourself permission to enjoy what you've achieved—and give yourself a lot of credit as well. You deserve it.

EMPTINESS

The feeling of emptiness does occur just on the cusp of fulfillment in love and work. When you feel empty, there's a void where a feeling ought to be. Most of us assume that as we begin to get what we want in love or work, content, happy, loving feelings will fill us up. And they often do. But periods of emptiness may alternate with these positive feelings.

As with postpartum depression, it is normal to feel empty when you get what you've wanted for a long time —a promotion, a baby, a house, a man. The emptiness occurs because now you must let go of years of struggling against frustrations and obstacles, and you no longer need to be fixated on your vision of the goal that has preoccupied you for many years. New projects and interests will fill in the void. But for the moment, emptiness is understandable.

If your past was filled with neglect, deprivation, or abuse of some kind, you might feel empty because, on the verge of having something better, you are leaving that painful past behind you. And although it was painful, leaving even an unpleasant childhood behind creates a void in you. Filling yourself up with new projects can be a constructive way to counteract the feeling of emptiness, or you might find a nurturing therapeutic group to help sustain you through this transitional period.

FEAR

When you have found security through success and/or love, you don't expect to feel afraid. But you may. "I am never afraid of what I know," said the English writer Anna Sewell. Know why you have these fears and they will lose their power. For example, once you have what you value most —a home, a man, a career you love, children—you may fear having it all taken away. The more you have, the more you have to lose; this is a truth we all know whether we are conscious of it or not. Yet it is unlikely that you will actually lose what you've achieved. Women who experience this fear to a debilitating extent often come from homes where their personal property was not protected. Louise is an example of this.

As a young child growing up in a large Italian family, Louise had few things of her own. Hand-me-downs and sharing were the rule for her. Her brothers were spoiled, though. Louise remembers several times that her mother insisted that she let her whining brothers play with dolls given to her as gifts, and how quickly they had broken them. The dolls were never replaced and her brothers were never punished. Louise grew up sure that nothing she loved could ever be hers for long. She feels this way now about her new apartment and her new man. In order to help herself, Louise can come to realize that she has power today that she never had as a child. If she needs to, she can fight to keep what she has attained.

Another fear could be called "performance anxiety," the fear that you will be unable to meet new expectations of you. You will blow it, lose it, forget what you know at the wrong moment, on the job or in a relationship. You may fear losing your various talents so much that you can't keep your position or keep a man. Whether or not these disasters could actually happen doesn't matter when you are worrying. It is important to remind yourself that these are only feelings, they are not reality, and they will stop eventually.

The fear of aging is the last fear I'll mention. Perhaps, like Peter Pan, you never wanted to grow up, but now you have success or love and suddenly you feel older. Obviously, deliberately keeping your life uneventful will not stop you from aging, but you might have felt younger before you "made it." You can tell yourself that you have to age anyway, and at least you're getting what you want—why be old and deprived? Your fears may upset you, but don't let them stop you from getting what you want.

GUILT

Since you are a woman you have most likely "gathered guilt like a young intern his symptoms, his certain evidence," as Anne Sexton wrote. Women are experts at finding any reason to feel guilty. But when you have achieved love or success, you are even more susceptible to feeling guilty than when you were far distant from your goals. Here are some of the most common sources of guilt when you are on the brink of having what you want.

Following a Different Path. It is likely that the work you are doing now and any romantic relationship you have are different from what your parents expected or what their life is like. Perhaps you want more intimacy, honesty, and equality in a relationship than your parents had. You want a career that will be far more important to you than the job your mother had. You have feelings that your parents told you, directly or indirectly, not to have—rage, jealousy, competitiveness, sexual needs—feelings they denied in themselves. There are many moments, especially during and after conversations with your parents, when you feel you're doing the wrong thing. When you are following a new path for yourself that is different from what your family planned for you, guilt is unavoidable, but unnecessary. Tell yourself that you have nothing to feel guilty about.

Winning. You may feel guilty because you are the one the boss picked to make the presentation or to take a prime business trip, or because you got the promotion, or because you're the one who met a great guy at a party while your friend didn't. Thus you feel guilty because you "won." You may also feel that there are others who are better, more qualified than you. You should realize that you're attacking yourself unnecessarily with untrue thoughts like this.

That Impostor Feeling. You continually feel you've misrepresented yourself when you're praised by anyone about anything. You think you're a phony. Thus you feel guilty unless you say that you're not that great, that you don't really know what you're doing. Even if you say this, you still feel like a phony, and you feel guilty about what you get. You wait to be "found out" by any new man in your life who likes you, or for the boss at work to discover the truth.

Feeling Undeserving. Now that you're close to having or actually have the career or money or man you want, or all of this, suddenly you feel guilty because you feel you're undeserving. After all, why should good things suddenly be happening to you? Perhaps you feel it came too easy, that it should have been harder for you. Tell yourself that you worked hard enough, and still do, and you deserve what you have.

Having More Than the Family Has. You feel guilty when all you've had is a good day but your father sounds like he hasn't even had that when you speak to him on the phone. When you actually have a man or success, the guilt can be overwhelming, especially if someone in your family is unhappy or unsuccessful. Perhaps your mother tells you how unhappy she is with your father, but your relationship is better than ever. Or you're about to go to Europe but your sister is out of a job. Immediately guilt sets in. The impact of your family on your love and work life is a strong force. Remind yourself that you deserve to have what you've worked for, even if the members of your family are still sabotaging themselves.

Leaving Home. Related to the above is the guilt that comes over you because you have left home. Some of us don't enjoy the homes of our own that we create, because our parents are not in them. Perhaps your parents never wanted you to leave. You've moved out to be with a man or to pursue your chosen career, but guilt still follows you. Tell yourself that you have a right to your own life!

These are the primary sources of the guilt you may feel on the brink of love or success: following a different path, winning, feeling like a phony, feeling undeserving, having more than your family has, and leaving home. Be aware of guilt, but don't let it rob you of your just rewards.

ANGER

Anger and success, anger and love. These words don't sound as though they belong together. Some women believe they have no right to feel angry if things are going well. But there are many reasons to feel angry as you near your goals. To her friends, Elizabeth seemed to "have it made," but she felt angry anyway. She had a marvelous career as a casting director, a new baby, and a seemingly attentive husband, but she felt angry for a reason that many women do: her work was never over. She had to work harder than ever to take care of the baby, herself, and her husband.

Having to prove yourself over and over again is very frustrating. Closely connected to this source of anger is another: you still have to take care of yourself financially. You may have had a fantasy that when the right man came along he would take over, or that you would make so much money that you wouldn't have to work regularly anymore. When neither happens, anger is unavoidable.

You may also be angry because now that you have what you wanted, you know what you missed out on for so many years. It doesn't seem fair that it took so long. You think about "all those wasted years." You may also be angry because you still want more. What you've got is suddenly not satisfying enough, yet you're tired of setting goals for yourself; you just want to be content.

Or you hope that one day your life will be trouble free, but you still get parking tickets, you pay more taxes than ever, and you find out that the man in your life is not always good for you. All of these conditions evoke angry feelings.

Finally, the anger you feel, consciously or not, may in some way be a product of your childhood. When you feel angry, think about whether you felt angry in a similar situation as a child. It will help to put it in perspective.

An American educator named Audre Lorde wrote, "There are so many roots to the tree of anger that sometimes the branches shatter before they bear." Don't let your very understandable anger shatter your branches once you have gained success or love. You have a right to feel angry, but find constructive ways to express it, and make sure to pamper yourself more than ever before.

LONELINESS

Loneliness means something different to each of us. One person may feel loneliness if she is far from friends and loved ones, while another may feel a degree of loneliness with family, at work, in any setting at all. It has been said that it is "lonely at the top," and you might think this only applies to the Howard Hughes types of the world, living alone in penthouses. But anyone who has moved up a notch in the world and changed her status in other's eyes will tell you that it can be lonely. Amy, for instance, was such an excellent assistant to Tim that she was made head of her own department. She felt excited about the opportunity, but she also felt lonely in her new office away from the others, with new responsibilities that she alone must handle.

Friendships can change as you find success or love, and this can also leave you feeling lonely. As you get what you want in a career, you may no longer want to listen to the chronic complaints of friends who apparently are stuck in unhappy, unfulfilling places. Finding new friends will happen over time, and you can be lonely until more fulfilling friendships appear. There's also a danger of feeling lonely when you're in a relationship, because you may cut yourself off from friends. Relying on one man to be your best and only friend is not only isolating but can be dangerous emotionally when the inevitable arguments occur between you, and you need nurturance from someone else.

There are deeper causes of loneliness also. In a romantic relationship you gain a mate, but deep down you can feel as if you are giving up your family. The unconscious "love affair" that Freud told us existed between all daughters and fathers is symbolically over. It is understandable that you feel lonely without your family. Even though they are there for you, the relationship is forever different.

Success and financial independence distances you from your family, which can result in feelings of loneliness, especially if you were financially dependent on them. Financially, you are leaving home. The feeling of loneliness will be especially severe if money was substituted for emotional closeness and nurturance. Without the "money connection," you may feel as if you are lost in space, with no connection to home at all. As with the other feelings, remember that loneliness is an emotional state and will come and go. Continue to reach out in your life for enjoyable people and experiences, and even if the feeling of loneliness is present, it will be powerless over you.

François Mauriac wrote, "The experience of happiness [is] the most dangerous, because all the happiness possible increases our thirst and the voice of love makes an emptiness, a solitude reverberate." On the brink of love or success, or after you have achieved them, emptiness, anxiety, disappointment, and all the feelings we have discussed can make you temporarily and understandably upset. Accept your feelings, then use your own ideas and the suggestions given throughout these pages to embrace your new life.

CHAPTER 10

▼▼

HOW TO SLAY YOUR OWN DRAGONS

▲▲

A *Ten-Point Plan*
▼▼▼▼▼▼▼▼▼▼▼▼▼▼▼▼▼▼▼▼▼▼▼▼

THE cure for self-sabotage cannot be easy or quick, because the problem is complex. Yet there *is* a cure, and it lies within you. Your emotional strength, which you do possess even though you may feel weak at the moment, and your motivation will be the ultimate weapons in your fight to have what you want in love and work. Jane Anderson, a professor of psychiatry at Harvard Medical School, agreed when she commented on what it was that allowed certain women to succeed despite adverse pressures: "What has made it possible for these women to keep going in the face of repeated, painful rebuffs . . . is their capacity . . . to provide positive feedback to themselves."

Providing positive feedback to yourself when you're depressed, financially in the red, or ill sounds like asking you to raft down the Colorado River after you've hiked the Rockies—you're already too spent and exhausted. But fresh supplies are on the way. In this chapter you'll find what you need to fight self-sabotage. Armed with the following ten-point plan, the skill will come with practice.

1. Imagine a realistic but promising vision of the life you want.

2. Practice self-observation with kindness and without self-blame.

3. Recognize and accept all your feelings.

4. Branch out psychologically from your family tree.

5. Make your physical health a priority.

6. Use visual imagery.

7. Create a support network.

8. Compliment yourself each time you risk change in your behavior.

9. Keep notes or make tapes of your thoughts and feelings.

10. Consider using some form of therapy to overcome self-sabotage.

No matter what form your self-sabotage takes, no matter whether you sabotage yourself in love or in work or both, it is possible to stop. The cure is not magical. You already have the tools; you just have to learn how to use them. We will now examine the ten points in greater detail. You won't need to use all these suggestions; use what works for you.

1. IMAGINE A REALISTIC BUT PROMISING VISION OF THE LIFE YOU WANT

In much the same way that the sun in the sky acts as a compass, a realistic vision of the love and success you want can keep you on track, despite the many pressures to become lost in self-sabotage. A realistic vision means that you include pitfalls and real hardships along with joys in this dream. Thucydides, the Greek philosopher, spoke of the courage it takes to have this kind of vision: "The bravest are surely those who have the clearest vision of what is before them, glory and danger alike, and yet notwithstanding, go out and meet it." It requires real courage to desire love and success but to see it without rose-colored glasses.

For instance, if the loving relationship you picture is filled with roses and kisses and daily flattery, you are mentally avoiding the unavoidable arguments, bad days, and negative feelings that inevitably occur in a relationship, and thus you may also be avoiding any but "perfect" men. On the other hand, if your vision of love is a sour one, without the sharing and sweetness, you will have little reason and less motivation to overcome self-sabotage and the other obstacles that can interfere with love.

Career achievement requires a realistic vision as well if you are to avoid self-sabotage. A recent *New Yorker* cartoon depicted a nineteen-year-old man socializing outside a bar, telling everyone that he was looking for a career where the money would roll in and he wouldn't have to work too much. This funny but unrealistic vision would hurt rather than help him. Similarly, setting your sights too low, telling yourself that the job you have is the only job you'll ever be able to get, also sabotages you.

It is important to have a vision of what you want, because self-made blockades of every type and obstacles and distractions created by others litter your path. Temporarily these will sidetrack you and may even stop you. But if you maintain a steadfast yet realistic vision of yourself involved in a life that satisfies you, you can always return to this vision no matter what obstacles you have to overcome.

2. PRACTICE SELF-OBSERVATION WITH KINDNESS AND WITHOUT SELF-BLAME

In order to understand what is meant by the above, imagine that a good friend has asked you for objective comments about her appearance. You want to be helpful, to be honest but constructive, not attacking or harsh. You tell her about the problems you've observed in a way that is kind. She's actually grateful and appreciates that you've taken the time to help her. Now place yourself in your friend's place and imagine giving yourself the same kind of feedback. This is self-observation with kindness and without self-blame, and it is a technique that you can use to help you change not only when you have an ongoing problem, but every day.

There are three special areas that you should focus on as you hone in with your microscope. By watching yourself in these specific areas, you'll see how your self-sabotage slows down just through objective observation.

Observe your particular pattern of self-sabotage. The most common patterns of self-sabotage that apply to love or work have been outlined in these chapters. Most likely the pattern of self-sabotage that you practice and that you should observe is one of the following:

▶ Emotional self-sabotage: passivity, anger, anxiety, or depression run your life.
▶ Self-sabotage through chronic financial disaster or through keeping yourself underpaid.
▶ Bodily self-sabotage through illness, fatigue, or accidents.
▶ Compulsions as a form of self-sabotage: addictions to food, alcohol, drugs, work.
▶ Sabotaging your love life by gravitating toward rejecting men, sticking with a man who mistreats you, or breaking up as you achieve success.

Observe coincidences. Instances of self-sabotage often just seem to happen, as if by coincidence, at the same time as positive events. Begin to observe, without self-blame, if this is true for you. For example, did a pattern of heavy drinking coincide with an important promotion? Did you meet a new man and then get sick? Did a financial problem or disaster occur on the heels of a joyful event, such as an engagement or the purchase of a new home? Have you felt more depressed or anxious ever since you were given a raise, came into some money, or found a better job or a better relationship? Did you suddenly start to overeat or smoke too much just when something good happened? Start to observe that there is nothing accidental when a good event is predictably followed by self-sabotage.

You can use your observations the way a scientist would use a seismosgraph to detect the vibrations of earthquakes. If you detect that bad things happen to you just after good ones, this is an indication of underlying feelings that may cause future emotional earthquakes unless you provide a valve so that the feelings can safely escape. If there is a coincidence between these good and bad events in your life, it means that you feel more conflict about having love or success than you may know. Become fully acquainted with these feelings, so that they will stop interfering and causing unpleasant "coincidences."

Observe your individual turnoff point. As previously defined, your individual turnoff point is the level of fulfillment in love or the amount of money or fame more than which, deep down, you feel you don't deserve. Take special notice of any area of your life in which you have felt chronically frustrated over a period of years. You have probably arived at your ITP. Perhaps you have been an assistant vice president in your company but can't seem to attain a vice presidency. Or you meet men but can't seem to find one who's willing to settle down. Or everything else in your life is fine, but money is a constant problem. In the first example, you would observe that your individual turn off point is at the assistant VP level; deep down you don't really feel entitled to be more successful. In the second case, your ITP is reached when you plan to marry; you may not feel entitled to a secure relationship. And in the third case, your turnoff point coincides with financial comfort; it's not really all right with you to have enough money to live comfortably. Your individual turnoff point does not have to last forever. Understand where this turnoff point came from: who told you that you don't deserve to have more? This will help as you struggle to overcome these deeply implanted negative messages. Turnoff points do not belong only to women; men arrive at stopping points in their lives as often as women do. It will help if you remember this when you encounter difficulties in relationships.

Do not blame yourself or try to immediately change anything based on your observations in any of these areas. Just use all the points in this chapter to aid you to *gradually* overcome self-sabotage.

3.   RECOGNIZE AND ACCEPT ALL YOUR FEELINGS

It is essential to monitor and recognize all your feelings when you are on the brink of love or success. Even a seemingly small accomplishment can mean more to you emotionally than you realize. A new car can be a symbol of success that can set off anxiety or fear in you. Buying a sexy new outfit or losing ten pounds may also make you feel anxious, if you have hidden fears about being attractive to men and this change has brought you a step closer to a relationship. Thus, to avoid self-sabotage, observe how you feel about all the changes in your life, even the small ones, and accept what you feel. Feelings that are unknown, buried deep within, can cause you to act out destructively. You then sabotage yourself to express these hidden feelings. All your feelings are healthy and normal.

Some feelings that women frequently experience on the brink of love or success are: anxiety, loneliness, fear, anger, guilt, disappointment and disillusionment, and emptiness. You may think of these feelings as the weak part of yourself, but feelings never weaken you. Only avoiding them will do that. Once you are willing to tolerate inner upset, you won't unconsciously need to create external turmoil by sabotaging yourself through accidents, illness, addictions, or financial disasters.

4.   BRANCH OUT PSYCHOLOGICALLY FROM YOUR FAMILY TREE

Because the manner in which we sabotage ourselves is unknowingly learned in the family, change requires separation from a psychological part of the family. Drug abuse, alcoholism, and physical violence are all destructive patterns that are commonly acknowledged to have been learned in the family. But every pattern that has been discussed—from passivity to perpetual illness, from destructive verbal anger to chronic financial crises—are also born out of family interactions. Searching in the family for the roots to passivity or chronic fatigue may be more difficult than pinpointing a history of alcoholism, but those roots are there. You may need to examine past generations; for example, was your grandmother a "sickly" woman who somatized her feelings too? Wherever the origins lie, finding them will make it easier for you to be understanding of yourself instead of critical. You can also see why a form of psychological separation from your family takes place when you stop sabotaging yourself.

Family members usually expect you to remain in your

old role with them. This can interfere with your growth. You can protect yourself from this negative force simply by being aware of it—or you can speak up.

Joan realized that she had been unable to form a lasting relationship with a man because she was so passive and self-demeaning. She ignored her own needs, took care of the men she became involved with, and was always scared that they would leave her. This pattern had originally formed between herself and her mother. Her mother still expected Joan to listen to her problems and ignored her daughter's needs. Joan eventually gained confidence in herself. During one of her mother's endless complaining sessions, Joan told her that listening to her complain was not going to be Joan's job anymore. Her mother stopped complaining to her and actually became enjoyable to be with. She began to realize she could not take Joan for granted. This change affected Joan's relationships with men, and soon she began meeting men who were interested in taking care of her, not just using her for her compassionate nature.

If you are willing to risk an emotional separation by becoming different than you were within your family, you may find, as Joan did, that your relationship with your family improves, once you reestablish who you are and how you want to be treated. Your determination to change old childhood patterns that have caused you to sabotage yourself and your willingness to be different, whatever that entails, are vitally important factors in overcoming self-destructiveness.

5.   MAKE YOUR PHYSICAL HEALTH A PRIORITY

It's generally agreed that day-to-day living creates stress that eventually affects our bodies. But when you are fighting self-sabotage, you are under a particularly high degree of stress. Thus, taking care of your body and your health should be a priority, so that you stay strong while you struggle to overcome your destructive patterns. Good health and a vital appearance also increases your confidence, which helps when you're in the midst of a personal emotional battle.

Fighting self-sabotage causes physical stress for a few reasons. Just admitting that you are sabotaging yourself produces stress, because you may feel that you need to fix the problem right away (which is impossible to do and should not be attempted). This stress may temporarily heighten whatever physical problems you have.

Physical symptoms can also develop when you begin to stop self-sabotage. When you stop drinking or eating compulsively, for example, you may experience anxiety, which can cause headaches, dizziness, or other symptoms. Or if you stop being passive and become more assertive, you may feel fear because of the unknown consequences. This fear could result in stomach problems, for instance. Another example is the woman who sabotages herself through explosive anger: she may feel stress when she starts to hold back her anger, even though she wants to and is doing this for very good reasons. The stress of holding herself back can then cause various physical symptoms, from a pounding heart to shortness of breath to headaches.

None of these physical symptoms are as bad as what will happen to you physically if you keep sabotaging yourself through overeating or being explosively angry. The new physical reactions you have when you stop sabotaging yourself will most likely fade away rapidly. But you should maintain good physical health by eating well and exercising, to help you withstand stress and its bodily repercussions. A two-mile walk, an exercise class, or a swim in a pool can do wonders to lessen anger or depression or anxiety.

Another reason you may need to separate psychologically from your family is to improve your eating habits and begin exercising. If your family is typical of many in that they eat too much, eat unhealthy foods, or don't exercise enough, you will find it harder to follow good health habits. Once you have improved your eating patterns and begun to exercise regularly, you may feel pressured during visits home to return to your old ways because of comments such as "I eat that and it never hurt me," or "Isn't that exercise thing a lot of nonsense anyway?" or "Are you trying to live forever?" One young woman who took diction lessons to get rid of a Brooklyn accent was made fun of by her family when she spoke without it. She soon gave up. Friends and colleagues often react similarly. Don't let these comments sabotage you. Make your physical well-being a priority in much the same way you overcome other problems: keep a vision in mind of the good health and fitness you want, despite the distractions. And don't blame yourself for temporary setbacks.

6. USE VISUAL IMAGERY

Visual imagery is a technique that has been used successfully in an amazing variety of areas. Competitive runners use it before a race, imagining every step of the course and the eventual victory. Cancer patients use this technique to fight the toxic cancer cells invading their bodies by envisioning the battle inside them, and the victory of the healthy cells. Dr. Carl Simonton and Stephanie Simonton have pioneered this technique in treating cancer patients. In their book, *Getting Well Again*, they describe how visual imagery works: "By forming an image, a person makes a clear mental statement of what she wants to happen. And by repeating the statement he or she soon comes to expect that the desired event will indeed occur." This image is a

very powerful tool in feeling better emotionally and physically. The more positive you are in visualizing yourself
defeating self-sabotage, the more likely it is that you will
get what you want in love and work.

Here are some steps to follow when you use visual
imagery to overcome self-sabotage. I have adapted these
from the techniques suggested by the Simontons.

> ▸ Visualize what you want to achieve in love or work.
> ▸ Visualize the ways in which you prevent yourself from
> getting what you want, such as being passive, overeating,
> spending compulsively, and getting into accidents.
> ▸ State firmly to yourself that you will not sabotage yourself
> in these ways.
> ▸ Visualize those who you feel have also been responsible
> for your self-sabotage or who are trying to defeat you.
> ▸ State firmly that you will not let them sabotage you or
> take away what you have worked for.
> ▸ Visualize yourself being the kind of person you want to
> be: assertive; slender; strong; wealthy; in love.
> ▸ Enjoy this improved picture of yourself.

Try to be as free and as positive as you can in your mental
imagery, without censoring whatever thoughts and images
come to mind as long as they are useful in defeating self-sabotage. When self-blame or other destructive thoughts interfere, stop yourself and start the steps over again. Do this for
a few minutes every day or at spontaneous moments whenever you feel you need help battling self-sabotage.

7. CREATE A SUPPORT NETWORK

A support network is composed of individuals or groups
that are on your side, ready to give you the strong, direct,
positive emotional communication you need when you feel

that you may be on the brink of self-sabotage or vulnerable to being sabotaged by others. Honest nurturance, sympathy, a vote of confidence in you and occasionally advice—this is what will help you past those days when each moment is a struggle.

A support network is effective because these "other voices" counteract the negative tapes that play in your mind, recorded there most probably during your childhood, as was discussed earlier. These negative voices tell you that you are wrong or bad, that you should drink or eat too much instead of reaching for help, that you should explode in anger at others instead of communicating your feelings constructively. The louder the voices of the support network are, the more they speak up to on your behalf, the less likely you are to sabotage yourself heeding the old voices. Before you automatically go to the refrigerator for ice cream, for example, you might stop and call someone from Overeaters Anonymous. This call will help you to quiet the voices telling you to eat.

Your support network should be made up of people who will listen to your feelings without condemning them. This gives you a chance to express the tension inside you so that you do not take self-destructive action.

Choose carefully those who will comprise your support network. Some colleagues might be supportive about work-related problems but not about your love life. Friends may be helpful about love but not about work. A family member may be in your fan club about your career but might not want to hear about your feelings. Do not expect to build a support network overnight, because compassionate and helpful individuals are rare and take time to find. Often the most reliable source of support may be found in therapeutic environments, such as groups like AA, or in traditional therapy. These sources of help will be discussed more fully later in this chapter.

8. COMPLIMENT YOURSELF EACH TIME YOU RISK CHANGE IN YOUR BEHAVIOR

When you change your behavior, even though it is for the better, there are always negative repercussions. All change thus involves a risk, even when the benefits outweigh the drawbacks. For example, you decide that you will stop smoking. A negative result is that you will be anxious and will not know what to do with your hands. You may gain weight at first. Positive results are that you will have more energy, increase your life expectancy, be less likely to come down with any number of illnesses, and eliminate the problems smoking creates in your relationships. Or you finally succeed in having more money. A negative result is that others will be jealous; a positive result of course will be a more comfortable and a calmer life.

These changes take courage, and you should feel proud of what you're doing. Pat yourself on the back whenever you take any step forward, no matter how small. If you're usually late to work by fifteen minutes and it's been a problem with the boss, compliment yourself the day you cut it to five. If depressed feelings usually keep you in bed in the morning but today you got up early and went jogging, compliment yourself. Complimenting yourself is especially important if you tend to dwell on your faults.

9. KEEP NOTES OR MAKE TAPES OF YOUR THOUGHTS AND FEELINGS

A written or spoken diary in which you record feelings when you're faced with troubling situations can help you to spot patterns of self-sabotage in your life. Reading over a few months' or a year's worth of notations can help you recognize a recurring problem. You will see that there is a pattern rather than an isolated series of bad-luck situations that are beyond your control.

Writing or speaking into a tape recorder can also help you "ventilate": it lets you release the feelings that make you prone to self-sabotage. It is a harmless way to feel better without taking any action. Decisions and actions should always be made when you feel better, *after* the strongest feelings have passed. In addition, writing or recording your thoughts is a way for you to practice expressing thoughts or feelings you are unused to communicating, like being assertive with a boss or constructively angry with your boyfriend.

There are numerous prerecorded cassettes available on the market today that can help you relax and build up your confidence. Use whatever you feel works to help you defeat self-sabotage.

10.   CONSIDER USING SOME FORM OF THERAPY TO OVERCOME SELF-SABOTAGE

Talking to caring friends, colleagues, or relatives can of course be therapeutic. But the type of therapy suggested here is one of the more traditional forms involving regular sessions, generally with a skilled professional or, in the case of the Anonymous groups, with members who have similar problems and who support each other.

Dorothy Semenow, a psychotherapist, in a speech called "Principles of Feminist Psychoanalysis," gave a wonderfully promising description of how therapy can help you defeat self-sabotage and achieve your goals:

> As early as possible in our analytic journey we try to sketch what kind of treasures the client wants to build into her life. True, she often comes to analysis caught up and spilling over with what is wrong. But buried in the suffering of those wrongs is

some notion of stunted rights. We uncover those rights lost in the client's yesterdays and add to them her hopes for her tomorrow.

One of the reasons that a regular form of therapy is important is that when you "spill over with what is wrong" in front of the same professional person or group regularly, you can ultimately spot your own self-destructive patterns. This is the first step before change occurs. Without this, your problems may just disguise themselves in a blur of repetitions. Therapy should also be a source of support and understanding that you can count on. Some professionals call it a type of "reparenting."

Individual or group therapy can provide a new, alternative voice to the sabotaging voices that may be in your head or may be coming from others. It can reduce your anxiety level and help you to feel taken care of. Therapy can also make functioning day to day easier and more productive and make major mishaps less likely. Therapy should help you express feelings and thoughts that have been hidden. When you choose a therapist or group, make sure that you feel understood when you are there; this is the best indication that you have found the right setting.

IN CONCLUSION

To paraphrase the philosopher Kierkegaard, "Life can only be understood backwards; but it must be lived forwards." He might have been giving a prescription for overcoming self-sabotage. You *can* move forward differently this time if you look back and discover the pattern of your self-sabotage, as Susan did. For many years Susan was an overworked, underpaid administrative assistant for a film company. Terrified of her bullying boss, she gave in to all his demands and asked for nothing in return. She was just as afraid of her boyfriend, who abused her as well. But she finally became motivated to change her situation when a new employee was given more responsibility and money than she. Friends and a support group helped her to see that she reacted to her boss and her boyfriend the same way she reacted to her father, acting like a scared child around them. With constant reminders to herself that she was *not* a child, and that her boss and her boyfriend were not her father, Susan began to speak up. She showed her considerable expertise in the business and asked for what she wanted. She is now producing short films and being treated far better by her man.

Susan saw that she was wasting the one life she had as an unknowing victim of the passive form of self-sabotage. She became determined to alter her pattern. As a result, her world will never be the same again.

It's never too late to change your life too by putting into practice any or all of these ten points, starting right now, and beginning to conquer self-sabotage. Or follow the steps used by any of the women in the chapters you have just read. All it takes is a decision; no expensive equipment or lessons or drastic personality changes are required. Being the terrific woman that you are, you have everything you need to get what you want in love and work. The fact that you have been willing to read through these pages, objectively evaluating the material that applies to you, means that you are far ahead of those who want to believe that bad luck is haunting them rather than realize they are sabotaging themselves.

Pushing yourself will not help; neither will blaming yourself. Allow your inner emotional self to change as it sees fit, with the gentle guidance of this program. Give yourself time to grow, gradually moving forward, and sometimes taking a step or two backward; you will surely be able to conquer or control your self-destructive habits. As you find what you want in love and work, new problems do arise, and the old sabotage syndrome can return briefly. But now you will have the skills needed to stop it quickly.

Slay your own dragons. Self-sabotaging thoughts and actions *are* dragons. They persecute you, destroy your confidence, and undermine your chances for love and success. Yet you don't need a knight in shining armor to gallop into your life to slay these dragons—and he can't do it without you anyway. You are the primary dragon-slayer; others can only stand by and shout encouragement. You have the white horse and the dragon-fighting equipment just waiting to be used so you can slay your own dragons and reap the rewards. Nothing is impossible; no self-destructive pattern is too awful, no habit is too ingrained to be overcome if you want things to be different.

Don't expect overnight success or rapid recoveries. There is no such thing. No one conquers a lifetime problem of self-sabotage without months or years of struggle. If you wake up one morning and say, "A-ha! My problem is over. I'm never going to do _____ again," be very suspicious. It just doesn't work that way. But do look for little changes and take pleasure and pride in them. They will become solid new habits to live by as time goes on. The big changes may come suddenly, when you least expect them. Don't jump into the future with your thoughts. Stay where you are with the small triumphs and savor them. There will be plenty more triumphs ahead—and plenty of dragons as well.

But this should not discourage you. Everyone's life is filled with dragons of their own making and ones created by others. Realize that you are not alone, and that the struggle for your eventual rewards can make those rewards even more meaningful when you get them. Knowing that others struggle also will bring you a sense of closeness to friends and family that you will find to be precious and perhaps even more to be cherished than the goals you set for yourself and finally achieve.

Meanwhile, you will find that slowly, month by month, there are fewer dragons ahead and they don't emerge from their caves as often. Occasionally they will flare up just to remind you of what you've conquered. But they will be easier to slay each time, and will die off more quickly than before. Techniques from the ten-point plan will become second nature to you as you swoop down upon your sabotaging thoughts and put them to rest. Any woman can become a dragon-slayer and overcome self-sabotage in her personal, social, and professional life, if she has the will. The battles and rewards are waiting. Saddle your white horse, and start today.